Unit Resource Guide
Unit 3
Exploring Multiplication

THIRD EDITION

KENDALL/HUNT PUBLISHING COMPANY
4050 Westmark Drive   Dubuque, Iowa 52002

A TIMS® Curriculum
University of Illinois at Chicago

 **UIC** The University of Illinois
at Chicago

The original edition was based on work supported by the National Science Foundation under grant
No. MDR 9050226 and the University of Illinois at Chicago. Any opinions, findings, and conclusions
or recommendations expressed in this publication are those of the author(s) and do not necessarily
reflect the views of the granting agencies.

Letter Home

Exploring Multiplication

Date: _____

Dear Family Member:

This unit is the first in a series of multiplication and division units distributed throughout the year. The units emphasize the development of multiplication concepts and their use in solving problems, rather than presenting multiplication simply as a series of isolated facts. Research has shown that this approach results in good achievement, good retention, and less time required to master computation skills.

In this unit, students work with multiplication in many settings. They make a class list similar to the one shown here and use it to create multiplication problems. Children will write stories involving multiplication such as, "There are eight legs on a spider. How many legs do six spiders have altogether?" Through exploration, your child will come to understand that there are several possible ways to solve such problems. As the unit progresses, ask your child about problems we worked on in class and some of the strategies used to solve them.

Groups of...	Item
two	mittens in a pair
three	corners on a triangle
four	seasons in a year
five	days of a school week

This list may be used by your child to think of multiplication stories.

Help your child at home with the following activities.

- **Group List.** Discuss with your child the list of groups the class made at school. Make up problems using items on the list. For example, while you are in the car, you might say, *There are four tires on each car, and I see six cars. How many tires in all?*

- **Multiplication Facts.** Take turns choosing multiplication facts to illustrate with stories and drawings. If your child chooses 4 × 5, you might draw a picture of four apples on five trees. Your child may draw a picture of four kittens in five baskets. Compare the stories and write number sentences for each: 4 × 5 = 20.

- **Subtraction Facts.** Help your child study the subtraction facts in Groups 3 and 4 using flash cards.

Thank you for your continued efforts to discuss real-world problems.

Sincerely,

_____

Carta al hogar

Investigando la multiplicación

Fecha: _____

Estimado miembro de familia:

Esta unidad es la primera de una serie de unidades relacionadas con la multiplicación y la división distribuidas durante todo el año. Las unidades ponen énfasis en el desarrollo de los conceptos de la multiplicación y en su uso para resolver problemas, en lugar de presentar la multiplicación como una serie de conceptos aislados. Las investigaciones muestran que con este enfoque se alcanzan mejores logros, buena retención y se requiere menos tiempo para dominar las habilidades de cálculo.

En esta unidad, los estudiantes trabajan con la multiplicación en una variedad de formas. Los estudiante harán una lista parecida a la que se muestra aquí y la usarán para crear problemas de multiplicación. Los estudiantes escribirán historias

Grupos de...	Objeto
dos	guantes en un par
tres	esquinas en un triángulo
cuatro	estaciones en un año
cinco	días en una semana escolar

Su hijo/a puede usar esta lista para pensar de historias de multiplicación.

que contengan multiplicaciones tales como, "Una araña tiene ocho patas. ¿Cuántas patas tendrán en total seis arañas?" A través de la exploración, su hijo/a entenderá que hay varias formas posibles de resolver estos problemas. Mientras la unidad avanza, pregúntele a su hijo/a acerca de problemas en los que trabajamos en la clase y alguna de las estrategias que los utilizadas para resolverlos.

Ayude a su hijo/a en casa con las siguientes actividades.

- **Lista de grupos.** Hable con su hijo/a acerca de la lista de grupos que la clase hizo en la escuela. Inventen problemas usando los objetos que están en la lista. Por ejemplo, mientras van en el automóvil, usted le puede decir, *"Cada automóvil tiene cuatro ruedas, y veo seis automóviles. ¿Cuántas ruedas hay en total?"*
- **Tablas de multiplicación.** Túrnese con su hijo/a para elegir multiplicaciones e ilústrenlas con historias y dibujos. Si su hijo/a escoge 4 3 5, usted puede hacer un dibujo de cuatro manzanas en cinco árboles. Su hijo/a puede hacer el dibujo de cuatro gatitos en cinco canastas. Comparen las historias y escriban las oraciones numéricas correspondientes a cada una: $4 \times 5 = 20$.
- **Restas básicas.** Ayude a su hijo/a a estudiar las restas básicas de los grupos 3 y 4 usando tarjetas.

Gracias por sus continuos esfuerzos para hablar sobre problemas de la vida real.

Atentamente,

_____

Unit 3
Exploring Multiplication

Unit 3

Outline
Exploring Multiplication

Unit Summary

Estimated Class Sessions

8

This is the first in a series of multiplication and division units distributed throughout the year. It begins a formal study of the concepts, applications, notation, and procedures involved in multiplying and dividing. Students solve problems about decorating T-shirts using the data on first names collected in Unit 1. Then they investigate things that come in 2s, 3s, 4s, etc., and use this information to solve problems such as finding the total number of wheels on five trucks. In another investigation, they use counters to divide numbers into groups in as many ways as possible.

Students write story problems to illustrate multiplication and division sentences. The ongoing activity, *Multiples on the Calendar,* introduces multiples and begins work with the multiplication facts. The DPP for this unit reviews the subtraction facts for Groups 3 and 4 and develops strategies for the multiplication facts for the fives and tens.

Major Concept Focus

- multiplication concepts
- multiplication stories
- investigating patterns
- multiplication as repeated addition
- multiplication number sentences
- subtraction facts review for Groups 3 and 4
- partitioning
- communicating problem-solving solutions
- multiplication facts strategies
- multiplication facts strategies for the 2s and 3s

Pacing Suggestions

This unit begins work with multiplication and division. Units that follow use the multiplication concepts developed in this unit to build additional skills and concepts. These skills and concepts are developed in a careful sequence as shown below. See the *Math Trailblazers*® Classroom section in the *Teacher Implementation Guide* for more information on pacing.

Unit 5:   Applying multiplication in a laboratory investigation (Lesson 3).
Unit 7:   Developing multiplication concepts including multiplication as repeated addition, multiplication on a number line, writing multiplication sentences, and representing multiplication using data tables and graphs.
Unit 8:   Using multiplication with map scales.
Unit 9:   Representing multiplication using data tables and graphs and solving multiplication problems involving mass.
Unit 10: Representing multiplication using data tables and graphs (Lesson 1) and solving problems involving multiplication (Lessons 1, 3, and 4).
Unit 11: Representing multiplication with arrays, building a multiplication table, developing strategies for multiplication facts, practicing multiplication facts using flash cards, and developing strategies for division through problem solving.
Unit 16: Solving multiplication and division problems involving volume (Lesson 2).
Unit 19: Developing strategies for multiplying one-digit by two-digit numbers and solving problems involving multiplication and division.
Unit 20: Representing multiplication using data tables and graphs, assessing the multiplication facts, and solving problems involving multiplication and division.

- Teach the units in the order they are written. Students will revisit important concepts and skills as they experience them in new contexts as the units progress. Units that do not contain significant multiplication content will include practice and review in the Daily Practice and Problems in the *Unit Resource Guide* and the Home Practice in the *Discovery Assignment Book.*

- Use the recommended session numbers for each lesson as a guide. It is not necessary to wait until students master each concept and skill as they will revisit them in later units and practice them in the Daily Practice and Problems and Home Practice throughout the year. Use the Assessment Indicators as a guide for the appropriate time to assess specific skills. The Assessment Indicators for all units are listed on the *Individual Assessment Record Sheet* in the Assessment section of the *Teacher Implementation Guide.*

- Lesson 6 *More T-Shirt Problems* is a series of word problems that are appropriate for homework. The lesson is also suitable for a substitute teacher since preparation is minimal.

Assessment Indicators

Use the following Assessment Indicators and the *Observational Assessment Record* that follows the Background section in this unit to assess students on key ideas.

A1. Can students interpret bar graphs?

A2. Can students represent multiplication problems using manipulatives and pictures?

A3. Can students create stories for multiplication sentences?

A4. Can students write number sentences for multiplication situations?

A5. Can students solve multiplication and division problems and explain their reasoning?

A6. Can students divide a set of objects into equal-size groups (with remainders) and represent the situation with a number sentence?

Unit Planner

Lesson Information	Supplies	Copies/Transparencies

Lesson 1

T-Shirt Factory Problems

URG Pages 22–29
SG Pages 32–33
DPP A–B

Estimated Class Sessions
1

Activity
Students use data from Unit 1 Lesson 1 *First Names* to solve problems about decorating T-shirts with their first names.

Math Facts
DPP Bit A provides practice with skip counting by ten.

Homework
Assign the following problem for homework: Your family is making T-shirts with their names on them. Draw pictures of all the T-shirts your family will need. If each letter costs 10 cents, how much will all the letters cost? Explain your solution.

Assessment
1. Assess students' abilities to solve problems and to work in groups by asking them to write a report of their group's strategies and solutions to Question 5 of the *T-Shirt Factory Problems*.
2. Use the *Observational Assessment Record* to document students' abilities to interpret bar graphs.

Supplies:
- connecting cubes or other counters
- calculators

Copies/Transparencies:
- 1 transparency of *T-Shirt Factory Problems* graph SG Page 32
- 1 copy of *Observational Assessment Record* URG Pages 11–12 to be used throughout this unit

Lesson 2

In Twos, Threes, and More

URG Pages 30–39
SG Pages 34–36
DAB Page 53
DPP C–F
HP Parts 1–2

Estimated Class Sessions
2

Activity
Students list items and then write multiplication problems about them.

Math Facts
DPP item C provides subtraction facts practice. Bit E reminds students to practice subtraction facts using the *Subtraction Flash Cards: Group 3*. Challenge F is a magic square problem.

Homework
1. Send home the *In Twos through Twelves* Activity Page. Families add new items to these lists.
2. Assign the Homework section in the *Student Guide*.
3. Collect one problem from each group and combine them into a class-generated homework assignment.
4. Assign Home Practice Part 1.
5. Students study the subtraction facts in Group 3 at home using their flash cards.

Assessment
1. Assess students' abilities to solve problems by asking them to solve a problem such as, *"How many corners are there on eight triangles?"* Note students' abilities to use words, pictures, or number sentences to show how they solved the problem.
2. Use Home Practice Part 2 as an assessment. Record students' abilities to solve problems involving multiplication on the *Observational Assessment Record*.

Supplies:
- 1 envelope for flash cards per student group
- several large index cards per student group, optional
- easel paper for making class lists
- tape for hanging class lists

	Lesson Information	Supplies	Copies/ Transparencies
Lesson 3 **Multiplication Stories** URG Pages 40–50 SG Pages 37–40 DPP G–J *Estimated Class Sessions* **2**	**Activity** Students illustrate multiplication problems with pictures and stories. **Math Facts** DPP Bit G provides practice with subtraction facts and develops mental math skills. Bit I reminds students to practice the subtraction facts in Group 4 using flash cards. **Homework** 1. Assign the homework problems in the *Student Guide*. 2. Students study the subtraction facts in Group 4 at home using their flash cards. **Assessment** Assess students' abilities to solve multiplication problems by asking them to write a story for a problem such as $8 \times \frac{1}{4}$, 10×9, or 20×3.	• connecting cubes or other counters • envelopes for flash cards • markers or crayons, optional	
Lesson 4 **Making Teams** URG Pages 51–58 DAB Pages 55–58 DPP K–L *Estimated Class Sessions* **1**	**Activity** Using counters as a model, students partition the students in a class into teams of equal size. Students write number sentences. **Math Facts** DPP Bit K develops multiplication math facts strategies. **Homework** Students complete *Groupings and Number Sentences for Ten* and the *Groupings and Number Sentences for Fifteen* Homework Pages in the *Discovery Assignment Book*.	• assortment of counters per student	• 1 transparency of *Class Teams Table* DAB Page 55
Lesson 5 **Multiples on the Calendar** URG Pages 59–65 DPP M–N HP Parts 3–4 *Estimated Class Sessions* **1**	**Activity** Students begin an ongoing activity translating calendar dates into number sentences that involve a product and a remainder. **Math Facts** DPP items M and N provide math facts practice. **Homework** Assign Home Practice Part 3. **Assessment** You can use Home Practice Part 4 as an assessment. Record students' abilities to create stories for multiplication sentences and write number sentences for multiplication situations on the *Observational Assessment Record*.	• beans or other counters, optional • large classroom calendar with space for writing number sentences	• 1 copy of *Calendar Multiplication* URG Page 64 per student

	Lesson Information	Supplies	Copies/Transparencies
Lesson 6 **More T-Shirt Problems** URG Pages 66–70 SG Page 41 DPP O–P *Estimated Class Sessions* **1**	**Activity** Students work on word problems involving multiplication and division. **Math Facts** DPP Bit O provides multiplication facts practice. **Assessment** 1. Use the *Observational Assessment Record* to record students' abilities to solve multiplication and division problems and explain their reasoning. 2. Transfer appropriate observations from the Unit 3 *Observational Assessment Record* to each student's *Individual Assessment Record Sheet*.	• calculators • connecting cubes or other counters	• 1 copy of *Individual Assessment Record Sheet* TIG Assessment section per student, previously copied for use throughout the year

Preparing for Upcoming Lessons

Allow students to explore base-ten pieces in a learning center before beginning Unit 4.

Connections

A current list of literature and software connections is available at *www.mathtrailblazers.com*. You can also find information on connections in the *Teacher Implementation Guide* Literature List and Software List sections.

Literature Connections
Suggested Titles

- Aker, Suzanne. *What Comes in 2s, 3s, and 4s?* Simon and Schuster, New York, 1992.
- Brenner, Martha. *Stacks of Trouble.* The Kane Press, New York, 2000.
- Calvert, Pam. *Multiplying Menace.* Charlesbridge Publishing, Watertown, MA, 2006.
- Clemson, Wendy and David. *Math Magic: Multiplying and Dividing.* Two-Can Publishing, Princeton, NJ, 2002.
- Giganti, Paul Jr. *Each Orange Had Eight Slices: A Counting Book.* Mulberry Books, New York, 1999. (Lesson 3)
- Long, Lynette. *Marvelous Multiplication: Games and Activities That Make Math Easy and Fun.* John Wiley & Sons, Inc., New York, 2000.
- Slobodkina, Esphyr. *Caps for Sale: A Tale of a Peddler, Some Monkeys and Their Monkey Business.* HarperTrophy, New York, 1997. (Lesson 4)
- Thompson, Lauren. *One Riddle, One Answer.* Scholastic Press, New York, 2001.

Software Connections

- *Kid Pix* allows students to create their own illustrations of objects in groups. (Lesson 3)
- *Math Concepts One . . . Two . . . Three!* provides exploration and practice with the four operations including work with magic squares.
- *Math Munchers Deluxe* includes practice with basic facts and factors and multiples in an arcade-like game.

- *Mighty Math Calculating Crew* poses short-answer questions about number operations and money skills.
- *National Library of Virtual Manipulatives* website (http://matti.usu.edu) allows students to work with manipulatives including geoboards, base-ten pieces, the abacus, and many others.
- *Number Facts Fire Zapper* provides practice with math facts.
- *Tenth Network: Grouping and Place Value* provides opportunities for students to group objects by 2s, 5s, and 10s.

Teaching All Math Trailblazers Students

Math Trailblazers lessons are designed for students with a wide range of abilities. The lessons are flexible and do not require significant adaptation for diverse learning styles or academic levels. However, when needed, lessons can be tailored to allow students to engage their abilities to the greatest extent possible while building knowledge and skills.

To assist you in meeting the needs of all students in your classroom, this section contains information about some of the features in the curriculum that allow all students access to mathematics. For additional information, see the Teaching the *Math Trailblazers* Student: Meeting Individual Needs section in the *Teacher Implementation Guide.*

Differentiation Opportunities in this Unit

Journal Prompts

Journal prompts provide opportunities for students to explain and reflect on mathematical problems. They can help both students who need practice explaining their ideas and students who benefit from answering higher order questions. Students with various learning styles can express themselves using pictures, words, and sentences. Teachers can alter journal prompts to suit students' ability levels. The following lessons contain a journal prompt:

- Lesson 1 *T-Shirt Factory Problems*
- Lesson 2 *In Twos, Threes, and More*
- Lesson 4 *Making Teams*
- Lesson 5 *Multiples on the Calendar*

DPP Challenges

DPP Challenges are items from the Daily Practice and Problems that usually take more than fifteen minutes to complete. These problems are more thought-provoking and can be used to stretch students' problem-solving skills. The following lessons have a DPP Challenge in them:

- DPP Challenge F from Lesson 2 *In Twos, Threes, and More*
- DPP Challenge L from Lesson 4 *Making Teams*
- DPP Challenge P from Lesson 6 *More T-Shirt Problems*

Extensions

Use extensions to enrich lessons. Many extensions provide opportunities to further involve or challenge students of all abilities. Take a moment to review the extensions prior to beginning this unit. Some extensions may require additional preparation and planning. The following lessons contain extensions:

- Lesson 5 *Multiples on the Calendar*
- Lesson 6 *More T-Shirt Problems*

Background
Exploring Multiplication

This unit is the first in a series of multiplication and division units distributed throughout the year. Building on their experiences in first and second grades, third-grade students will begin a more formal study of the concepts, applications, notation, and procedures of multiplying and dividing. As recommended in the NCTM's *Principles and Standards for School Mathematics,* the units will emphasize the development of concepts and the use of computation to solve problems. Students will investigate multiplication and division by solving problems and sharing solutions and strategies with one another. Your role is to help students connect their thinking about multiplication and division to the appropriate mathematical symbols and to help them become more efficient in their estimation and computation. Additional background on problem solving can be found in the TIMS Tutor: *Word Problems* in the *Teacher Implementation Guide.*

In this unit, multiplication is introduced in a variety of settings so students will have different ways to access the mathematics. For more information, see the Teaching the *Math Trailblazers* Student: Meeting Individual Needs section in the *Teacher Implementation Guide.* As students solve many types of problems, introduce the use of multiplication sentences linking the symbols to students' informal procedures (Carpenter, Carey, and Kouba, 1990, p. 127).

In later units, students will continue to investigate multiplication by collecting data and looking for patterns in data tables and graphs. These patterns provide a context for building multiplication tables and developing strategies for learning the basic facts. Students will also explore the patterns involved in using multiples of ten to facilitate estimation and to check the reasonableness of their results. When students are familiar with underlying concepts and skills, they will write and solve story problems involving larger numbers. These problems act as a catalyst for developing an understanding of two-digit by one-digit multiplication. Calculators are used to assist students in their investigations and problem solving involving large numbers and complex calculations.

For information on the study of the multiplication facts in Grade 3, see the Daily Practice and Problems Guide for this unit and the *Grade 3 Facts Resource Guide.* For more information, see the TIMS Tutor: *Math Facts.*

"Students with conceptual understanding know more than isolated facts and methods. They understand why a mathematical idea is important and the kinds of contexts in which it is useful. They have organized their knowledge into a coherent whole, which enables them to learn new ideas by connecting those ideas to what they already know. Conceptual understanding also supports retention. Because facts and methods learned with understanding are connected, they are easier to remember and use, and they can be reconstructed when forgotten."

From the National Research Council *Adding It Up: Helping Children Learn Mathematics,* 2001, p. 118.

Resources

- Burns, Marilyn. *A Collection of Math Lessons from Grades 3 through 6.* The Math Solution Publications, New Rochelle, NY, 1987.

- Burns, Marilyn. *Math by All Means: Multiplication Grade 3.* The Math Solution Publications, New Rochelle, NY, 1991.

- Carpenter, T.P., D.A. Carey, and V.L. Kouba, "A Problem-Solving Approach to the Operations." In J.N. Payne (Ed.). *Mathematics for the Young Child.* National Council of Teachers of Mathematics, Reston, VA, 1990.

- Carpenter, T.P., E. Fennema, M.L. Franke, L. Levi, and S.E. Empson. *Children's Mathematics: Cognitively Guided Instruction.* Heinemann, Westport, CT, 1999.

- Isaacs, A.C., and W.M. Carroll. "Strategies for Basic-Facts Instruction." *Teaching Children Mathematics,* 5 (9), pp. 508–515, 1999.

- National Research Council. "Developing Proficiency with Whole Numbers." In *Adding It Up: Helping Children Learn Mathematics.* J. Kilpatrick, J. Swafford, and B. Findell, eds. National Academy Press, Washington, DC, 2001.

- Post, Thomas R. (Ed.) *Teaching Mathematics in Grades K through 8: Research-Based Methods.* Allyn and Bacon, Needham Heights, MA, 1992.

- *Principles and Standards for School Mathematics.* National Council of Teachers of Mathematics, Reston, VA, 2000.

- Thornton, C.A. "Emphasizing Thinking Strategies in Basic Fact Instruction." *Journal for Research in Mathematics Education,* 9 (3), pp. 214–227, 1978.

- Thornton, C.A. "Strategies for the Basic Facts." *Mathematics for the Young Child,* pp. 133–151, J.N. Payne, ed. National Council of Teachers of Mathematics, Reston, VA, 1990.

Observational Assessment Record

A1 Can students interpret bar graphs?

A2 Can students represent multiplication problems using manipulatives and pictures?

A3 Can students create stories for multiplication sentences?

A4 Can students write number sentences for multiplication situations?

A5 Can students solve multiplication and division problems and explain their reasoning?

A6 Can students divide a set of objects into equal-size groups (with remainders) and represent the situation with a number sentence?

A7 _____

Name	A1	A2	A3	A4	A5	A6	A7	Comments
1.								
2.								
3.								
4.								
5.								
6.								
7.								
8.								
9.								
10.								
11.								
12.								
13.								

Name	A1	A2	A3	A4	A5	A6	A7	Comments
14.								
15.								
16.								
17.								
18.								
19.								
20.								
21.								
22.								
23.								
24.								
25.								
26.								
27.								
28.								
29.								
30.								
31.								
32.								

Unit 3

Daily Practice and Problems
Exploring Multiplication

A DPP Menu for Unit 3

Two Daily Practice and Problems (DPP) items are included for each class session listed in the Unit Outline. A scope and sequence chart for the DPP is in the *Teacher Implementation Guide*.

Icons in the Teacher Notes column designate the subject matter of each DPP item. The first item in each class session is always a Bit and the second is either a Task or Challenge. Each item falls into one or more of the categories listed below. A menu of the DPP items for Unit 3 follows.

N Number Sense	⊠ Computation	🕐 Time	⬡ Geometry
A, B, D, H, J	A, F, J, L, P	D, J, L	
⁵⁄₇ Math Facts	$ Money	⚖ Measurement	▨ Data
A, C, E–G, I, K, M–O	J, L, O, P		

Practicing the Subtraction Facts

DPP items in this unit provide a review of the subtraction facts for Group 3 ($10 - 4$, $9 - 4$, $11 - 4$, $10 - 8$, $11 - 8$, $9 - 5$, $10 - 6$, $11 - 6$, and $11 - 5$) and Group 4 ($10 - 7$, $9 - 7$, $11 - 7$, $10 - 2$, $9 - 2$, $9 - 3$, $10 - 3$, $11 - 3$, $9 - 6$). Facts in these groups can be solved by making a ten, using a ten, counting back, or counting up.

DPP items E and I ask students to use flash cards to study these subtraction facts and update their *Subtraction Facts I Know* charts. *Subtraction Flash Cards: Groups 3* and *4* can be found in the *Discovery Assignment Book* following the Home Practice. See DPP items C, G, and N for practice with these facts.

For information on the practice and assessment of subtraction facts in Grade 3, see the Lesson Guide for Unit 2 Lesson 7 *Assessing the Subtraction Facts*.

Developing Strategies for the Multiplication Facts

DPP items in this unit develop strategies for the multiplication facts for the fives and tens. See DPP items A, K, M, and O for work with these facts.

Students develop strategies for the multiplication facts in Units 3–10. The multiplication facts are practiced and assessed in Units 11–20. See the schedule in Figure 1. For more information on the study of the multiplication facts in Grade 3, see the Daily Practice and Problems Guide for Unit 11. For a detailed explanation of our approach to learning and assessing the math facts in Grade 3, see the *Grade 3 Facts Resource Guide* and for information for Grades K–5, see the TIMS Tutor: *Math Facts* in the *Teacher Implementation Guide.*

Unit	Multiplication Facts
3	Develop strategies for the 5s and 10s
4	Develop strategies for the 2s and 3s
5	Develop strategies for the square numbers
6	Develop strategies for the 9s
7	Develop strategies for the last six facts: $4 \times 6, 4 \times 7, 4 \times 8, 6 \times 7, 6 \times 8, 7 \times 8$
8	Develop strategies for the 2s, 5s, and 10s
9	Develop strategies for the 3s, 9s, and squares
10	Develop strategies for the last six facts: $4 \times 6, 4 \times 7, 4 \times 8, 6 \times 7, 6 \times 8, 7 \times 8$
11	Practice and assess the 5s and 10s
12	Practice and assess the 2s and 3s
13	Practice and assess the square numbers
14	Practice and assess the 9s
15	Practice and assess the last six facts
16	Practice and assess the 2s, 5s, and 10s
17	Practice and assess the 3s and 9s
18	Practice and assess the square numbers
19	Practice and assess the last six facts
20	Assess all the multiplication fact groups

Figure 1: *Distribution of the multiplication facts in Grade 3*

 **Daily Practice and Problems**

Students may solve the items individually, in groups, or as a class. The items may also be assigned for homework. The DPPs are also available on the Teacher Resource CD.

Student Questions	Teacher Notes
(A) Number of Toes How many toes are in your classroom?	**TIMS Bit** Students can use counting strategies to find the answer.
(B) Number of Students There are 47 students in the third grade. The number 47 is . . . A. 3 more than _____ B. 3 less than _____ C. 10 more than _____ D. 10 less than _____ E. about half of _____ F. about twice _____	**TIMS Task** After students write down their answers, let them discuss their strategies, as well as their answers. A. 44 B. 50 C. 37 D. 57 E. A number between 90 and 100 F. 23, 24, or 25

Student Questions	Teacher Notes

C Subtraction: Making a Ten

Write the answers to these problems.

1. 10 − 8 =

2. 11 − 8 =

3. 9 − 5 =

4. 10 − 4 =

5. 11 − 4 =

6. 9 − 4 =

7. 10 − 6 =

8. 11 − 6 =

9. 11 − 5 =

TIMS Bit

This bit reviews the facts in *Group 3* of the *Subtraction Flash Cards*. Ask students to describe strategies. Children are often comfortable with sums of 10 (e.g., 2 + 8, 6 + 4). They can use these facts to find differences from 10 (10 − 8 = 2, 10 − 4 = 6) or to find similar facts such as 11 − 4.

1. 2   2. 3

3. 4   4. 6

5. 7   6. 5

7. 4   8. 5

9. 6

D Calculator Counting with 10s

Work with a partner. One partner will count. The other will time the counting partner.

A. Predict how long it will take to count by 10s to 500. Use a calculator to count by 10s to 500. Say the numbers quietly to yourself. How long did it take?

B. Use a calculator to count by 10s backward from 500 to 0. Say the numbers quietly to yourself. What patterns do you see?

TIMS Task

Pressing 10 + 10 = = = on a calculator with a constant function will cause the calculator to count by 10s.

To count backward from 500 on a calculator, press
500 − 10 = = = =.

Counting by tens forward and backward will help students use counting strategies when adding and subtracting multiples of 10.

E Subtraction Flash Cards: Group 3

1. With a partner, sort the flash cards into three stacks: Facts I Know Quickly, Facts I Know Using a Strategy, and Facts I Need to Learn.

2. Update your *Subtraction Facts I Know* chart. Circle the facts that you answered quickly. Underline those you knew by using a strategy. Do nothing to those you still need to learn.

TIMS Bit

Pass out *Subtraction Flash Cards: Group 3.* After students sort, they should update the *Subtraction Facts I Know* chart. Students can take the cards for Group 3 home to practice with their families.

F A Magic Square with Tens

Complete the magic square using the numbers 10, 20, 30, 40, 50, 60, 70, 80, and 90. Each row, column, and diagonal must have a sum of 150.

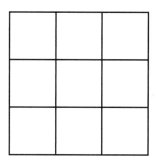

TIMS Challenge

This is the same magic square as the one in *Yü the Great* except the numbers are multiples of 10. One possible solution:

80	10	60
30	50	70
40	90	20

If students need a hint, remind them that the 5 was in the middle of the magic square in the story.

Student Questions	Teacher Notes

G Subtraction: Making a Ten Again

Do these problems in your head. Write only the answers.

1. $10 - 7 =$

2. $11 - 7 =$

3. $9 - 7 =$

4. $10 - 3 =$

5. $11 - 3 =$

6. $9 - 3 =$

7. $100 - 20 =$

8. $90 - 20 =$

9. $9 - 6 =$

TIMS Bit

This bit reviews the facts in *Group 4* of the *Subtraction Flash Cards.*

Ask students to describe the strategies they used to solve these problems. Possible strategies include making a ten, thinking addition, and using related facts. Knowing $10 - 3 = 7$ helps solve $9 - 3 = 6$. Knowing $10 - 2 = 8$ helps solve $100 - 20 = 80$. Class discussion can help students choose efficient strategies.

1. 3   2. 4
3. 2   4. 7
5. 8   6. 6
7. 80   8. 70
9. 3

H Number of Bikes

There are 51 bikes at the school. The number 51 is . . .

A. 3 more than _____

B. 3 less than _____

C. 10 more than_____

D. 10 less than _____

E. about half of _____

F. about twice _____

TIMS Task

After students write down their answers, let them discuss their strategies, as well as their answers.

A. 48
B. 54
C. 41
D. 61
E. 100
F. 25

Student Questions	Teacher Notes

I **Subtraction Flash Cards: Group 4**

1. With a partner, sort the flash cards into three stacks: Facts I Know Quickly, Facts I Know Using a Strategy, and Facts I Need to Learn.

2. Update your *Subtraction Facts I Know* chart. Circle the facts that you answered quickly. Underline those you knew by a strategy. Do nothing to those you still need to learn.

TIMS Bit $\frac{5}{\times 7}$

Pass out the *Subtraction Flash Cards: Group 4*. Students sort the cards with a partner and update their *Subtraction Facts I Know* charts. Students can take their flash cards for Group 4 home to practice with a family member.

J **Sam's and Sasha's Savings**

1. Sam wants a book that costs $1.50. He can save 25¢ a week. How many weeks will he need to save to have enough for the book?

2. Sasha is saving for a Chicago Bulls poster that costs $4.50. He has $2.50 now and can save 10¢ a week. How long will it take him to save enough for the poster?

TIMS Task Ⓝ Ⓢ Ⓒ ✳

Ask students to share their solutions. Possible solutions include:

1. Skip counting by 25 up to 150 and counting the number of 25s.

25¢, 50¢, 75¢, $1, $1.25, $1.50

1 2 3 4 5 6 wks.

2. $4.50 − $2.50 = $2.00. Since there are 20 dimes in $2, it will take Sasha 20 weeks to save enough money for the poster.

K **Pumpkins in Wagons**

This story problem was written by a third-grade student:

There are ten wagons and three pumpkins in each wagon. How many pumpkins are there? Solve the problem.

TIMS Bit $\frac{5}{\times 7}$

30 pumpkins

One good strategy for solving this problem is to draw a picture of the story.

Student Questions	Teacher Notes

L   **Sally's and Sara's Savings**

1. Sally is saving for a pair of gym shoes that cost $45. Right now she has $13. She can save $2 a week. How many weeks will Sally need to save until she has enough money for her shoes? How many months?

2. Sara wants a jump rope that costs $8. She has only $1.50 now. She can save $1 each week. How long will it be until Sara has enough money for her jump rope?

TIMS Challenge

There are many possible strategies for solving the problems. Make sure students explain their solutions.

1. 16 weeks or about 4 months

2. Sara needs to save $6.50 ($8 − $1.50 = $6.50). Since she can save $1 each week, it will take 7 weeks to save the entire amount.

M   **Making Groups**

You have thirty-seven beans. Make groups of five. Write a number sentence that shows your work. Don't forget about leftover beans.

TIMS Bit

Students might write:

$7 \times 5 + 2 = 37$

or

$5 \times 7 + 2 = 37$

N   **Subtraction Stories**

1. Write a story and draw a picture for 10 − 4.

2. Write a story and draw a picture for 11 − 4.

TIMS Task

Stories will vary.

Student Questions	Teacher Notes

◉ Frank's Hamburger Stand

A hamburger and a soda cost $5.00 at Frank's Hamburger Stand. Derek, Sean, Karl, and Cindy each ordered a hamburger and a soda. What is the total cost? Write a number sentence to show your work.

TIMS Bit $\boxed{\$}$ $\boxed{\times \frac{5}{7}}$

$5.00 + $5.00 + $5.00 + $5.00 = $20.00

or

4 × $5.00 = $20.00

ⓟ Camping Trip

The Cub Scouts are planning a camping trip. There are fifteen boys in the den. Two fathers will also go. They plan to rent four-person tents for $20 each. They will also rent two-person canoes for $10 each. What is the total cost of the canoes and tents?

TIMS Challenge $\boxed{\$}$ ▨

The Cub Scouts will need 5 tents and 9 canoes. The total cost is $190.

T-Shirt Factory Problems

Lesson Overview

Estimated Class Sessions

1

The lab *First Names* in Unit 1 Lesson 1 introduced a graph based on students' first names. In this activity, students work in groups to solve problems that build on their work from the lab. First, groups solve a problem concerning the number of letters in their first names. Then, a story about a fictitious class that is decorating T-shirts with the students' first names serves as the context for a series of problems. Students will use all four operations, but the problems lend themselves to the use of multiplication.

Key Content

- Interpreting bar graphs.
- Exploring multiplication through problem solving.
- Using patterns in data to solve problems.
- Solving problems involving multiplication.

Key Vocabulary

- Multiplication number sentence

Math Facts

DPP Bit A provides practice with skip counting by ten.

Homework

Assign the following problem for homework: Your family is making T-shirts with their names on them. Draw pictures of all the T-shirts your family will need. If each letter costs 10 cents, how much will all the letters cost? Explain your solution.

Assessment

1. Assess students' abilities to solve problems and to work in groups by asking them to write a report of their group's strategies and solutions to Question 5 of the *T-Shirt Factory Problems*.
2. Use the *Observational Assessment Record* to document students' abilities to interpret bar graphs.

Curriculum Sequence

Before This Unit

Students explored multiplication in Grade 2 Unit 12.

After This Unit

Students will further explore multiplication concepts in Grade 3 Units 7, 9, 10, 11, and 19

Materials List

Supplies and Copies

Student	Teacher
Supplies for Each Student • connecting cubes or other counters • calculator	**Supplies**
Copies	**Copies/Transparencies** • 1 transparency of *T-Shirt Factory Problems* graph (*Student Guide* Page 32) • 1 copy of *Observational Assessment Record* to be used throughout this unit (*Unit Resource Guide* Pages 11–12)

All blackline masters including assessment, transparency, and DPP masters are also on the Teacher Resource CD.

Student Books
T-Shirt Factory Problems (*Student Guide* Pages 32–33)

Daily Practice and Problems and Home Practice
DPP items A–B (*Unit Resource Guide* Page 15)

Note: Classrooms whose pacing differs significantly from the suggested pacing of the units should use the Math Facts Calendar in Section 4 of the *Facts Resource Guide* to ensure students receive the complete math facts program.

Assessment Tools
Observational Assessment Record (*Unit Resource Guide* Pages 11–12)

Daily Practice and Problems

Suggestions for using the DPPs are on page 27.

A. Bit: Number of Toes (URG p. 15) [N] [✖] [5 x 7]

How many toes are in your classroom?

B. Task: Number of Students [N]
(URG p. 15)

There are 47 students in the third grade. The number 47 is . . .

A. 3 more than ___

B. 3 less than ___

C. 10 more than ___

D. 10 less than ___

E. about half of ___

F. about twice ___

Review the data from the Unit 1 Lesson 1 *First Names*.

Teaching the Activity

Part 1 Our Class

Ask students to imagine that all the students in class will decorate T-shirts with their first names. Each student should then draw a picture of a T-shirt and write his or her first name on the shirt. Below the T-shirt, each student should write the number of letters in his or her name.

Have students form groups based on the number of letters in their names. For example, all students with four letters in their first names will form one group. Ask each group to solve the following problem:

• *Every student in your group will sew his or her name on a T-shirt. At a craft store, letters cost 10 cents each. How much will it cost to buy all the letters for your group?*

Groups should carefully record their solutions and strategies so they can report to the rest of the class. If a group is having trouble, remind them that they may use pictures, counters, calculators, or other tools to help them. Although this problem lends itself to multiplication, groups may choose to use other strategies, such as repeated addition or skip counting. Encourage groups to use number sentences in their reports.

As students share their solutions with the rest of the class, highlight the various strategies. Children with different learning styles benefit from seeing different strategies used to solve problems. See the Teaching the *Math Trailblazers* Student: Meeting Individual Needs section of the *Teacher Implementation Guide* for more information. In a discussion, emphasize the link between multiplication sentences and student solutions. For example, there were five students who each had four-letter names. One student said, "Each name costs 40 cents. This can be written like $10 + 10 + 10 + 10 = 40$ cents or it can also be written as $4 \times 10 = 40$ cents. Since our group has five people, the total cost is $40 + 40 + 40 + 40 + 40 = 200$ cents or two dollars."

Another student said, "Our group has 4×5 or 20 letters. Since each letter is 10 cents, the total cost is twenty tens. I skip counted by tens twenty times and got 200 cents or two dollars." You may need to review or introduce multiplication number sentences.

Journal Prompt

Write a journal entry describing how your group found the cost of letters for all the people in your group.

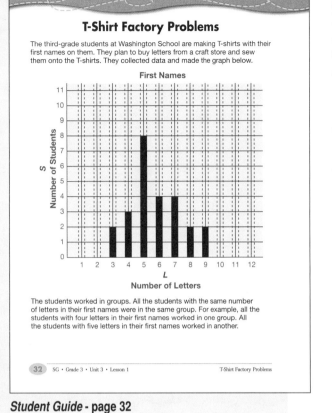

T-Shirt Factory Problems

The third-grade students at Washington School are making T-shirts with their first names on them. They plan to buy letters from a craft store and sew them onto the T-shirts. They collected data and made the graph below.

First Names

Number of Students (S) vs Number of Letters (L)

The students worked in groups. All the students with the same number of letters in their first names were in the same group. For example, all the students with four letters in their first names worked in one group. All the students with five letters in their first names worked in another.

Student Guide - page 32

Use the graph to solve the following problems. Explain your solution. Try to use a number sentence to show your thinking.

1. **A.** Levi, Mara, and John have four letters in their names. Draw a picture of their three T-shirts with their names on them.

   B. How many letters will they have to buy altogether?

2. **A.** How many students have eight letters in their names?

   B. How many letters will these students need to buy in order to write all their names on all their T-shirts?

3. **A.** How many students have six letters in their names?

   B. How many letters are needed to write all their names on all their T-shirts?

4. Each letter costs 10 cents. How much will it cost to buy all the letters for the group with three letters in their names?

5. How much will it cost to buy all the letters for the group with five letters in their names?

6. **A.** Which group will need more letters: the group with five letters in their names or the group with seven letters?

   B. How many more letters will that group need?

7. How much will the letters cost for the group with nine letters?

8. How many letters are needed to make T-shirts for the whole class?

Student Guide - page 33 *(Answers on p. 29)*

Introduce the graph on the *T-Shirt Factory Problems* Activity Pages. With a transparency of this page, ask questions like:

- *What are the labels for the horizontal axis and the vertical axis?* (*L,* Number of Letters; *S,* Number of Students)

- *Which numbers on the graph indicate the number of students?* (The numbers along the vertical axis.)

- *Which numbers on the graph indicate the number of letters in the first names?* (The numbers along the horizontal axis.)

- *How many students have four letters in their first names?* (3 students)

- *How many students have seven letters in their first names?* (4 students)

- *How many more students have five letters than four letters?* (5 students)

- *There were eight students in one of the groups. How many letters do these students have in their names?* (5 letters)

Once students are familiar with the graph, divide them into groups of three or four and ask them to solve the problems in the *Student Guide.*

Encourage students to solve the problems in more than one way as a means of checking their answers. Tell the groups that they should be ready to explain their methods to the class. They should write down their solutions, using number sentences whenever possible. During class discussion, emphasize the use of varied approaches and connect them to multiplication where appropriate.

Math Facts

DPP Bit A provides practice with skip counting by ten.

Homework and Practice

- Task B develops number sense.
- Assign the following problem for homework: Your family is making T-shirts with their names on them. Draw pictures of all the T-shirts your family will need. If each letter costs 10 cents, how much will all the letters cost? Explain your solution.

Assessment

- Assess students' abilities to solve problems and to work in groups by asking them to write a report of their group's strategies and solutions to *Question 5* of the *T-Shirt Factory Problems.* Students can work collaboratively or individually. Often, students' journeys to identical solutions will differ. Students may give their reports orally, answering questions from the class. An alternative is to evaluate the reports by asking students to exchange written reports and ask questions. If the writing is clear and complete, partners should have no trouble understanding the solution.
- Document students' abilities to interpret bar graphs using the *Observational Assessment Record.*

At a Glance

Math Facts and Daily Practice and Problems
DPP Bit A provides practice with skip counting by ten and Task B develops number sense.

Part 1. Our Class
1. Review the data from the *First Names* lab in Unit 1.
2. Describe the class project centered around the number and cost of letters that need to be purchased for the T-shirts.
3. Have students form groups based on the number of letters in their first names.
4. Groups solve the problem.
5. Groups report their solutions and methods.

Part 2. T-Shirt Factory Problems
1. Introduce the graph on the *T-Shirt Factory Problems* Activity Pages in the Student Guide.
2. Ask questions to familiarize students with the graph.
3. Student groups solve the *T-Shirt Factory Problems.*
4. Groups share their solutions and their methods.
5. Emphasize the use of varied approaches and connect them to multiplication where appropriate.

Homework

Assign the following problem for homework: Your family is making T-shirts with their names on them. Draw pictures of all the T-shirts your family will need. If each letter costs 10 cents, how much will all the letters cost? Explain your solution.

Assessment

1. Assess students' abilities to solve problems and to work in groups by asking them to write a report of their group's strategies and solutions to **Question 5** of the *T-Shirt Factory Problems.*
2. Use the *Observational Assessment Record* to document students' abilities to interpret bar graphs.

Answer Key is on page 29.

Notes:

Student Guide (p. 33)

Solution strategies will vary. Students may use counters, pictures, as well as number sentences. Possible strategies and number sentences are shown.

I. **A.** Pictures will vary.

    B. $4 + 4 + 4 = 12$ letters or
        $3 \times 4 = 12$ letters

2. **A.** 2 students

    B. $8 + 8 = 16$ letters or
        $2 \times 8 = 16$ letters

3. **A.** 4 students

    B. $6 + 6 + 6 + 6 = 24$ letters or
        $4 \times 6 = 24$ letters

4. 2 students $\times$ 3 letters = 6 letters
Skip count by 10¢ six times to find the cost of 6 letters: 10, 20, 30, 40, 50, 60¢.
$6 \times 10¢ = 60¢$

5. 8 students have 5 letters.
Skip count by 5 eight times:
$5 + 5 + 5 + 5 + 5 + 5 + 5 + 5 = 40$ letters
40 letters $\times$ 10¢ = 400¢ or $4.

6. **A.** The group with seven letters needs $7 + 7 + 7 + 7 = 28$ letters, so the group with five letters needs more letters. (See **Question 5.**)

    B. $40 - 28 = 12$ letters

7. The letters for one shirt cost $9 \times 10¢ = 90¢$.
$90¢ + 90¢ = 180¢$ or $1.80

8. $6 + 12 + 40 + 24 + 28 + 16 + 18 = 144$ letters. Using a calculator is an appropriate strategy for this problem.

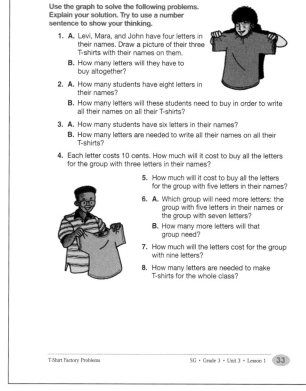

Use the graph to solve the following problems. Explain your solution. Try to use a number sentence to show your thinking.

1. **A.** Levi, Mara, and John have four letters in their names. Draw a picture of their three T-shirts with their names on them.
   B. How many letters will they have to buy altogether?

2. **A.** How many students have eight letters in their names?
   B. How many letters will these students need to buy in order to write all their names on all their T-shirts?

3. **A.** How many students have six letters in their names?
   B. How many letters are needed to write all their names on all their T-shirts?

4. Each letter costs 10 cents. How much will it cost to buy all the letters for the group with three letters in their names?

5. How much will it cost to buy all the letters for the group with five letters in their names?

6. **A.** Which group will need more letters: the group with five letters in their names or the group with seven letters?
   B. How many more letters will that group need?

7. How much will the letters cost for the group with nine letters?

8. How many letters are needed to make T-shirts for the whole class?

T-Shirt Factory Problems   SG • Grade 3 • Unit 3 • Lesson 1   33

Student Guide - page 33

Lesson 2

In Twos, Threes, and More

Lesson Overview

Students make lists of things that come in twos, threes, fours, and so on, up to twelves. For instance, eyes and bicycle wheels come in twos. Students write multiplication problems based on items in this list. They solve these problems using various strategies and multiplication sentences to express their answers. Discussing their solution strategies is an important part of this lesson.

Key Content

- Representing multiplication with manipulatives and pictures.
- Writing multiplication number sentences.
- Communicating solutions verbally and in writing.
- Creating word problems involving multiplication.
- Connecting multiplication and repeated addition.
- Connecting multiplication and addition of equal-sized groups.

Math Facts

DPP item C provides subtraction facts practice. Bit E reminds students to practice subtraction facts using the *Subtraction Flash Cards: Group 3.* Challenge F is a magic square problem.

Homework

1. Send home the *In Twos through Twelves* Activity Page. Families add new items to these lists.
2. Assign the Homework section in the *Student Guide.*
3. Collect one problem from each group and combine them into a class-generated homework assignment.
4. Assign Home Practice Part 1.
5. Students study the subtraction facts in Group 3 at home using their flash cards.

Assessment

1. Assess students' abilities to solve problems by asking them to solve a problem such as, *"How many corners are there on eight triangles?"* Note students' abilities to use words, pictures, or number sentences to show how they solved the problem.
2. Use Home Practice Part 2 as an assessment. Record students' abilities to solve problems involving multiplication on the *Observational Assessment Record.*

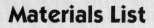

Materials List

Supplies and Copies

Student	Teacher
Supplies for Each Student Group • envelope for flash cards • several large index cards, optional	**Supplies** • easel paper for making class lists • tape for hanging class lists
Copies	**Copies/Transparencies**

All blackline masters including assessment, transparency, and DPP masters are also on the Teacher Resource CD.

Student Books

In Twos, Threes, and More (*Student Guide* Pages 34–36)
Subtraction Flash Cards: Group 3 (*Discovery Assignment Book* Pages 49–50)
In Twos through Twelves (*Discovery Assignment Book* Page 53)

Daily Practice and Problems and Home Practice

DPP items C–F (*Unit Resource Guide* Pages 16–17)
Home Practice Parts 1–2 (*Discovery Assignment Book* Page 46)

Note: Classrooms whose pacing differs significantly from the suggested pacing of the units should use the Math Facts Calendar in Section 4 of the *Facts Resource Guide* to ensure students receive the complete math facts program.

Assessment Tools

Observational Assessment Record (*Unit Resource Guide* Pages 11–12)

Daily Practice and Problems

Suggestions for using the DPPs are on pages 35–36.

C. Bit: Subtraction: Making a Ten
(URG p. 16)

1. $10 - 8 =$ 2. $11 - 8 =$
3. $9 - 5 =$ 4. $10 - 4 =$
5. $11 - 4 =$ 6. $9 - 4 =$
7. $10 - 6 =$ 8. $11 - 6 =$
9. $11 - 5 =$

D. Task: Calculator Counting
with 10s (URG p. 16)

Work with a partner. One partner will count.
The other will time the counting partner.

A. Predict how long it will take to count by
   10s to 500. Use a calculator to count by
   10s to 500. Say the numbers quietly to
   yourself. How long did it take?

B. Use a calculator to count by 10s backward
   from 500 to 0. Say the numbers quietly to
   yourself. What patterns do you see?

E. Bit: Subtraction Flash Cards:
Group 3 (URG p. 17)

1. With a partner, sort the flash cards into three
   stacks: Facts I Know Quickly, Facts I Know
   Using a Strategy, and Facts I Need to Learn.

2. Update your *Subtraction Facts I Know* chart.
   Circle the facts that you answered quickly.
   Underline those you knew by using a strategy.
   Do nothing to those you still need to learn.

F. Challenge: A Magic Square
with Tens (URG p. 17)

Complete the magic square using the numbers
10, 20, 30, 40, 50, 60, 70, 80, and 90. Each row,
column, and diagonal must have a sum of 150.

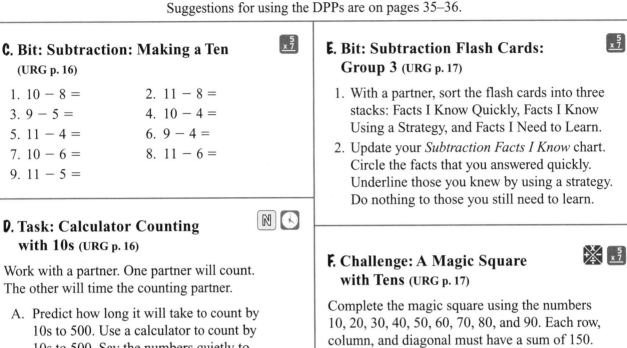

Part 1 Things That Come in Groups

Begin by involving the class in a discussion:

- *How many shoes are there on six children?*
- *How many wheels are there on five cars?*
- *How many arms are there on three octopuses?*

Use larger numbers as students seem ready for them.

As students answer the questions, ask how they arrived at their answers. Encourage others to share additional solution methods. As students describe their methods, write number sentences that summarize their results on the board.

For instance, one way to solve the question *"How many shoes are there on six children?"* is to use repeated addition: $2 + 2 + 2 + 2 + 2 + 2 = 12$ shoes. This problem can also be solved by skip counting by twos. In one class, students suggested acting out the skip counting: each stood up one at a time while the class counted their shoes—2, 4, 6, 8, 10, 12. When discussing the solutions, focus on the fact that the shoes can be counted in six groups of two. Introduce the related multiplication sentence: $6 \times 2 = 12$ shoes.

After discussing these problems, ask the class to turn to *In Twos, Threes, and More* in the *Student Guide.* Talk about the questions in the book, and ask them for a multiplication sentence for each problem. As the multiplication sentences are given, write them on the board.

TIMS Tip

Creating lists can pose several pitfalls. Children may list too many examples of one type, such as body parts. Other items are not good examples because they are unique—there is only one set of seven continents. Items such as families can cause confusion because they come in different sizes.

In Twos, Threes, and More

34   SG • Grade 3 • Unit 3 • Lesson 2   In Twos, Threes, and More

Student Guide - page 34

Use the picture to answer the following questions.

1. There are four clocks in the picture. Each clock has three hands. How many hands are there on all the clocks? How did you find out?

2. The clock hands come in four groups of three hands. Other items in the picture also come in groups. Some of them are listed below. How many of each item are there altogether? Explain how you found your answers.
   A. Tennis balls in packages
   B. Eyes on dolls
   C. Legs on horses
   D. Teacups in tea sets
   E. Wheels on motorcycles

3. Tina the Tennis Pro bought five packages of tennis balls.
   A. How many tennis balls did she buy altogether?
   B. Write a multiplication sentence that shows your answer.

4. Mary received two Tea Time sets for her birthday. How many people can she invite to a tea party?

5. Shelly's family has three watches. One watch has two hands. Each of the other two watches has three hands. How many hands are on the watches altogether? Explain how you got your answer.

6. Alex bought one of the horses. How many legs are on the horses in the store now?

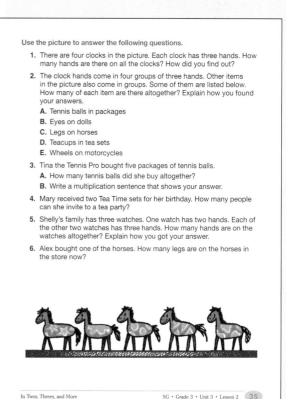

In Twos, Threes, and More   SG • Grade 3 • Unit 3 • Lesson 2   35

Student Guide - page 35 (Answers on p. 38)

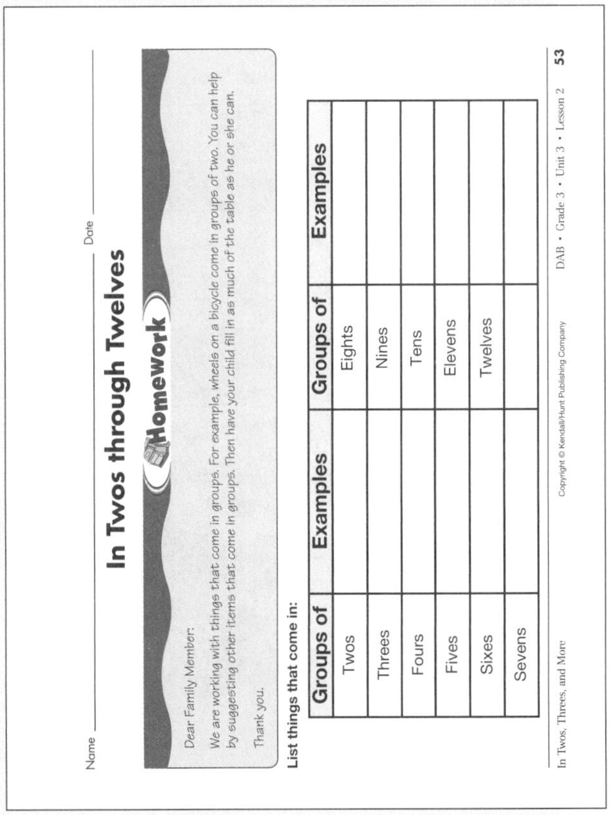

The left image content (rotated activity page):

Name _____ Date _____

In Twos through Twelves

Homework

Dear Family Member:

We are working with things that come in groups. For example, wheels on a bicycle come in groups of two. You can help by suggesting other items that come in groups. Then have your child fill in as much of the table as he or she can.

Thank you.

List things that come in:

Groups of	Examples		Groups of	Examples
Twos			Eights	
Threes			Nines	
Fours			Tens	
Fives			Elevens	
Sixes			Twelves	
Sevens				

Copyright © Kendall/Hunt Publishing Company

In Twos, Threes, and More

DAB • Grade 3 • Unit 3 • Lesson 2   53

Journal Prompt

Choose something from your class list that comes in sixes. Write a multiplication story problem about it. Use a number sentence to show the answer.

Ask students to form small groups to brainstorm lists of things that come in twos through twelves. They can use the *In Twos through Twelves* Activity Page in the *Discovery Assignment Book* to record their items using words or pictures. Tell them their lists will be used to make problems similar to those you have been discussing. Examples of items they might list are in the table below.

Things That Come In Groups

Groups of...	Item
two	mittens in a pair
three	corners on a triangle
four	seasons in a year
five	days in a school week
six	cans in a six-pack of soda pop
seven	hours in a school day
eight	legs on a spider
nine	players on a baseball team
ten	digits on a calculator
eleven	players on a football team
twelve	inches in a foot

Figure 2: *Students create lists of things that come in groups.*

Discuss the lists, then combine them into a single class list that you record on easel paper and save for the next day. This list will serve as the basis for the multiplication problems students will create. Suggest that students ask their families to help them think of some additions to the list.

Part 2 **Writing Problems and Using Number Sentences**

Begin the second day by looking at the class list again and asking whether the students have any additions to make. Choose an object from the list and pose a multiplication question. Draw a picture on the board to illustrate the question, write the problem in words, and introduce a multiplication sentence for the problem. Figure 3 provides an example.

How many seasons are there in three years?
3 X 4 = 12 seasons

Figure 3: *An example of a drawing and number sentence for a multiplication problem*

After modeling this type of problem and solution a few times, ask student groups to use their lists to write similar problems of their own. Ask them to record the problem in words on one side of the paper (or index card) and their illustration, solution, and multiplication sentence on the other. Groups can then pose questions for the rest of the class or exchange their problems with other groups. These problems can also be collected and assigned as homework or used as a problem of the day.

Content Note

At this point, do not place too much emphasis on the order of the factors in a multiplication sentence. It is standard practice to associate the number sentence $3 \times 4 = 12$ with the sentence *3 groups of 4 equal 12*. However, some children might write $4 \times 3 = 12$. Since multiplication is commutative, this is acceptable.

Math Facts

DPP item C provides subtraction facts practice. Bit E reminds students to practice facts using the *Subtraction Flash Cards: Group 3*. Challenge F is a magic square problem.

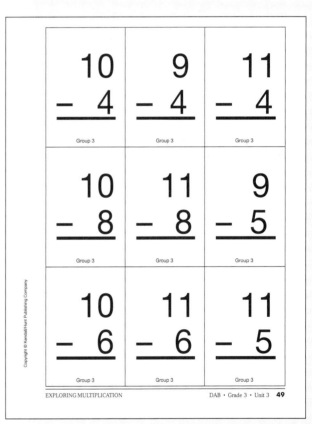

Discovery Assignment Book - page 49

<table>
<tr><td>

Homework

1. **A.** How many people are in your family?
   B. How many toes does your family have altogether? Explain how you got your answer.
   C. Complete a multiplication sentence like the following that shows your answer.

   _____ × 10 = _____

2. **A.** How many chairs are at the table where you eat?
   B. How many legs are there on all the chairs at your table? Explain how you found your answer.
   C. Write a multiplication sentence that shows your answer.

   _____ × 4 = _____

3. **A.** Kim has eight stuffed animals. How many eyes do her stuffed animals have altogether? Explain how you got your answer.
   B. Write a multiplication sentence that shows your answer.

4. **A.** Joanne bought 4 six-packs of juice boxes as a treat for her soccer team. How many juice boxes did she bring?
   B. Write a multiplication sentence that shows your answer.

5. **A.** Hot dog buns come in packs of eight. How many buns are in three packs?
   B. Write a number sentence that shows your answer.

6. **A.** How many days are in 4 weeks?
   B. Write a number sentence that shows your answer.

7. **A.** Draw a picture of something that comes in a group that you find in your home.
   B. Write a multiplication sentence that describes your picture.

36   SG • Grade 3 • Unit 3 • Lesson 2   In Twos, Threes, and More

</td></tr>
</table>

Student Guide - page 36 *(Answers on p. 38)*

<table>
<tr><td>

Name _____ Date _____

Unit 3 Home Practice

PART 1

1. **A.** 9 – 5 = _____   2. **A.** 90 – 50 = _____
   B. 11 – 7 = _____   **B.** 110 – 70 = _____
   C. 10 – 2 = _____   **C.** 100 – 20 = _____

3. When the school bus arrived at school, Carla counted the number of people on it. There were twenty-four people. This was sixteen more than when she first got on. How many people were on the bus when Carla got on?

   _____
   _____
   _____
   _____

PART 2

Five third-grade students are competing in a math contest. They each bought a shirt with "math" printed on the front. Show how you solved the problem.

1. How many letters were printed in all?

   _____
   _____
   _____

2. If each letter costs 10¢, how much did it cost to have "math" printed on all five shirts?

   _____
   _____
   _____

46   DAB • Grade 3 • Unit 3   EXPLORING MULTIPLICATION

</td></tr>
</table>

Discovery Assignment Book - page 46 *(Answers on p. 39)*

Homework and Practice

- For Task D, students time how long it takes to count by 10s to 500 on a calculator.

- Send home the *In Twos through Twelves* Activity Page in the *Discovery Assignment Book*. Encourage families to add new items to the lists the students generated in class.

- Assign the homework problems in the *Student Guide*.

- Collect one problem from each group and combine them into a class-generated homework assignment.

- Assign Home Practice Part 1. Students use subtraction facts to solve problems.

- Students take home the *Subtraction Flash Cards: Group 3* and the list of facts they need to study so they can practice with a family member.

Assessment

- Assess students' problem-solving abilities by asking them to solve a problem such as, "How many corners are there on eight triangles?" Ask them to describe in words or a picture how they solved the problem. Encourage students to include a number sentence.

- Home Practice Part 2 can be used to assess students' abilities to solve multiplication problems. Encourage students to use pictures and number sentences to explain their solutions. Record students' progress on the *Observational Assessment Record*.

Answers for Parts 1 and 2 of the Home Practice are in the Answer Key at the end of this lesson and at the end of this unit.

Estimated Class Sessions

2

At a Glance

Math Facts and Daily Practice and Problems

DPP item C provides subtraction facts practice. For Task D, students skip count by 10s on calculators. Bit E reminds students to practice subtraction facts using the *Subtraction Flash Cards: Group 3*. Challenge F is a magic square problem.

Part 1. Things That Come in Groups

1. Pose questions such as *"How many shoes are there on six children?"*
2. As students describe their methods for solving the problems, write number sentences on the board.
3. Students discuss the questions in *In Twos, Threes, and More* in the *Student Guide.*
4. In groups, students list things that come in groups on the In *Twos through Twelves* Activity Page in the *Discovery Assignment Book.*

Part 2. Writing Problems and Using Number Sentences

1. Choose items from the *In Twos through Twelves* Activity Page and pose a multiplication question. Use pictures, words, and number sentences to describe the problem.
2. Students choose items from the list and write similar problems.
3. Groups exchange problems in class. Problems can be collected and assigned as homework.

Homework

1. Send home the *In Twos through Twelves* Activity Page. Families add new items to these lists.
2. Assign the Homework section in the *Student Guide.*
3. Collect one problem from each group and combine them into a class-generated homework assignment.
4. Assign Home Practice Part 1.
5. Students study the subtraction facts in Group 3 at home using their flash cards.

Assessment

1. Assess students' abilities to solve problems by asking them to solve a problem such as, *"How many corners are there on eight triangles?"* Note students' abilities to use words, pictures, or number sentences to show how they solved the problem.
2. Use Home Practice Part 2 as an assessment. Record students' abilities to solve problems involving multiplication on the *Observational Assessment Record.*

Answer Key is on pages 38–39.

Notes:

Use the picture to answer the following questions.

1. There are four clocks in the picture. Each clock has three hands. How many hands are there on all the clocks? How did you find out?

2. The clock hands come in four groups of three hands. Other items in the picture also come in groups. Some of them are listed below. How many of each item are there altogether? Explain how you found your answers.
   A. Tennis balls in packages
   B. Eyes on dolls
   C. Legs on horses
   D. Teacups in tea sets
   E. Wheels on motorcycles

3. Tina the Tennis Pro bought five packages of tennis balls.
   A. How many tennis balls did she buy altogether?
   B. Write a multiplication sentence that shows your answer.

4. Mary received two Tea Time sets for her birthday. How many people can she invite to a tea party?

5. Shelly's family has three watches. One watch has two hands. Each of the other two watches has three hands. How many hands are on the watches altogether? Explain how you got your answer.

6. Alex bought one of the horses. How many legs are on the horses in the store now?

In Twos, Threes, and More   SG • Grade 3 • Unit 3 • Lesson 2   35

Student Guide - page 35

Student Guide (p. 35)

1. 12 hands; count them; skip count by threes; multiply $4 \times 3 = 12$ hands

2. A. 24 tennis balls; $8 \times 3 = 24$; skip count by threes

   B. 22 eyes; $11 \times 2 = 22$; $11 + 11 = 22$; skip count by twos

   C. 20 legs; $5 \times 4 = 20$; skip count by twos

   D. 18 tea cups; $6 + 6 + 6 = 18$; $6 \times 3 = 18$; skip count by threes

   E. 16 wheels; $2 \times 8 = 16$; skip count by twos

3. A. 15 tennis balls

   B. $5 \times 3 = 15$

4. 12 people; $2 \times 6 = 12$

5. 8 hands; $2 \times 3 = 6$ hands on two watches 2 more hands on the third watch; 8 hands in all

6. 16 legs, $4 \times 4 = 16$ or $20 - 4 = 16$

Homework

1. A. How many people are in your family?
   B. How many toes does your family have altogether? Explain how you got your answer.
   C. Complete a multiplication sentence like the following that shows your answer.
   _____ × 10 = _____

2. A. How many chairs are at the table where you eat?
   B. How many legs are there on all the chairs at your table? Explain how you found your answer.
   C. Write a multiplication sentence that shows your answer.
   _____ × 4 = _____

3. A. Kim has eight stuffed animals. How many eyes do her stuffed animals have altogether? Explain how you got your answer.
   B. Write a multiplication sentence that shows your answer.

4. A. Joanne bought 4 six-packs of juice boxes as a treat for her soccer team. How many juice boxes did she bring?
   B. Write a multiplication sentence that shows your answer.

5. A. Hot dog buns come in packs of eight. How many buns are in three packs?
   B. Write a number sentence that shows your answer.

6. A. How many days are in 4 weeks?
   B. Write a number sentence that shows your answer.

7. A. Draw a picture of something that comes in a group that you find in your home.
   B. Write a multiplication sentence that describes your picture.

36   SG • Grade 3 • Unit 3 • Lesson 2   In Twos, Threes, and More

Student Guide - page 36

Student Guide (p. 36)

Homework

1. A. Answers will vary; we use 5 family members as an example.

   B. Answers will vary; 50 toes, counting by fives, multiply

   C. Answers will vary; $5 \times 10 = 50$ toes

2. A. Answers will vary; 5 chairs

   B. Answers will vary; 20 legs, skip count by fours, multiply

   C. Answers will vary; $4 \times 5 = 20$ legs

3. A. 16 eyes

   B. $8 \times 2 = 16$ eyes

4. A. 24 juice boxes

   B. $4 \times 6 = 24$ juice boxes

5. A. 24 buns

   B. $3 \times 8 = 24$ buns

6. A. 28 days

   B. $4 \times 7 = 28$ days

7. A. Answers will vary.

   B. Answers will vary.

Discovery Assignment Book (p. 46)

Home Practice*

Part 1

1. A. 4
   B. 4
   C. 8
2. A. 40
   B. 40
   C. 80
3. $24 - 16 = 8$ people

Part 2

Strategies will vary.

1. $5 \times 4 = 20$ letters
2. $20 \times \$0.10 = \$2.00$

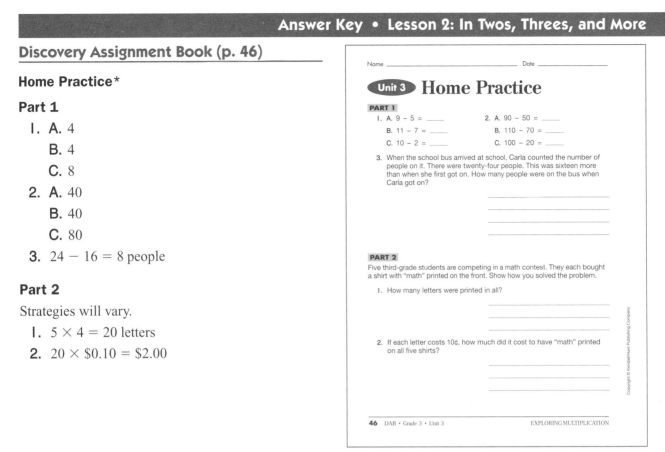

Name _____ Date _____

Unit 3 Home Practice

PART 1

1. A. $9 - 5 = $ _____
   B. $11 - 7 = $ _____
   C. $10 - 2 = $ _____
2. A. $90 - 50 = $ _____
   B. $110 - 70 = $ _____
   C. $100 - 20 = $ _____

3. When the school bus arrived at school, Carla counted the number of people on it. There were twenty-four people. This was sixteen more than when she first got on. How many people were on the bus when Carla got on?

   _____
   _____
   _____

PART 2

Five third-grade students are competing in a math contest. They each bought a shirt with "math" printed on the front. Show how you solved the problem.

1. How many letters were printed in all?

   _____
   _____

2. If each letter costs 10¢, how much did it cost to have "math" printed on all five shirts?

   _____
   _____

46 DAB · Grade 3 · Unit 3   EXPLORING MULTIPLICATION

Discovery Assignment Book - page 46

Discovery Assignment Book (p. 53)

In Twos through Twelves

See Lesson Guide 2 for a sample list.†

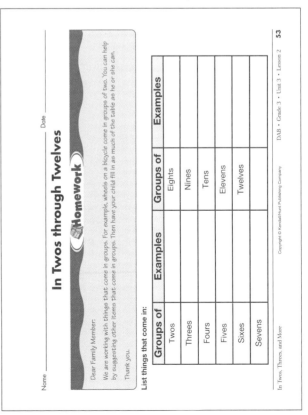

Discovery Assignment Book - page 53

*Answers for all the Home Practice in the *Discovery Assignment Book* are at the end of the unit.
†Answers and/or discussion are included in the Lesson Guide.

Lesson 3

Multiplication Stories

Lesson Overview

Students continue to explore multiplication by drawing pictures and writing stories to illustrate multiplication problems such as 7×8, 4×20, and $4 \times \frac{1}{2}$.

Key Content

- Representing multiplication with pictures and words.
- Writing number sentences for multiplication situations.
- Solving multiplication problems and explaining the reasoning.

Math Facts

DPP Bit G provides practice with subtraction facts and develops mental math skills. Bit I reminds students to practice the subtraction facts in Group 4 using flash cards.

Homework

1. Assign the homework problems in the *Student Guide*.
2. Students study the subtraction facts in Group 4 at home using their flash cards.

Assessment

Assess students' abilities to solve multiplication problems by asking them to write a story for a problem such as $8 \times \frac{1}{4}$, 10×9, or 20×3.

Materials List

Supplies and Copies

Student	Teacher
Supplies for Each Student • connecting cubes or other counters • envelopes for flash cards • markers or crayons, optional	**Supplies**
Copies	**Copies/Transparencies**

All blackline masters including assessment, transparency, and DPP masters are also on the Teacher Resource CD.

Student Books
Multiplication Stories (*Student Guide* Pages 37–40)
Subtraction Flash Cards: Group 4 (*Discovery Assignment Book* Pages 51–52)

Daily Practice and Problems and Home Practice
DPP items G–J (*Unit Resource Guide* Pages 18–19)

Note: Classrooms whose pacing differs significantly from the suggested pacing of the units should use the Math Facts Calendar in Section 4 of the *Facts Resource Guide* to ensure students receive the complete math facts program.

Daily Practice and Problems

Suggestions for using the DPPs are on page 44.

G. Bit: Subtraction: Making a Ten Again $\boxed{\frac{5}{\times 7}}$
(URG p. 18)

Do these problems in your head. Write only the answers.

1. $10 - 7 =$ 2. $11 - 7 =$
3. $9 - 7 =$ 4. $10 - 3 =$
5. $11 - 3 =$ 6. $9 - 3 =$
7. $100 - 20 =$ 8. $90 - 20 =$
9. $9 - 6 =$

I. Bit: Subtraction Flash Cards: Group 4 $\boxed{\frac{5}{\times 7}}$
(URG p. 19)

1. With a partner, sort the flash cards into three stacks: Facts I Know Quickly, Facts I Know Using a Strategy, and Facts I Need to Learn.

2. Update your *Subtraction Facts I Know* chart. Circle the facts that you answered quickly. Underline those you knew by a strategy. Do nothing to those you still need to learn.

H. Task: Number of Bikes (URG p. 18) $\boxed{N}$

There are 51 bikes at the school. The number 51 is . . .

A. 3 more than ___

B. 3 less than ___

C. 10 more than___

D. 10 less than ___

E. about half of ___

F. about twice ___

J. Task: Sam's and Sasha's Savings (URG p. 19) $\boxed{N}$ $\boxed{\$}$ $\boxed{\bigcirc}$ $\boxed{\times}$

1. Sam wants a book that costs $1.50. He can save 25¢ a week. How many weeks will he need to save to have enough for the book?

2. Sasha is saving for a Chicago Bulls poster that costs $4.50. He has $2.50 now and can save 10¢ a week. How long will it take him to save enough for the poster?

First, students read the *Multiplication Stories* Activity Pages in the *Student Guide.* These pages show pictures and descriptions that illustrate a multiplication problem.

After the class has read and discussed the pages, ask them to draw pictures and write their own stories about these problems. Encourage students to include multiplication sentences with their stories. After students finish drawing and writing, ask them to share their stories with the rest of the class.

Questions 7A–7C involve only one-digit factors and serve as an introduction to the multiplication facts. *Question 7D,* like the problem 4 × 20, involves one factor that is a multiple of ten. To investigate multiplication in multiples of ten, ask students to describe any patterns they find as they solve these problems.

Questions 7E and 7F include one factor that is a fraction, similar to the last example in *Multiplication Stories.* Traditionally, children multiply whole numbers for a long period of time before they are introduced to multiplication with fractions. By learning multiplication exclusively with whole numbers, children develop the erroneous notion that the product is always larger than its factors—in short, that multiplying always makes "bigger" numbers. By including fractions in these problems, students learn early that multiplication can also produce smaller numbers. Problems with fractions can be solved using strategies similar to those used to solve the first problems—drawing pictures and using repeated addition.

TIMS Tip

Students work well in pairs for this activity. Pairs can use counters in creating their multiplication stories. For more information on grouping students, see the Building the *Math Trailblazers* Classroom section of the *Teacher Implementation Guide.*

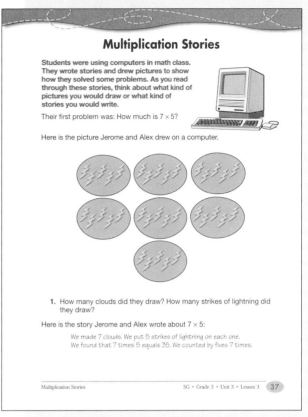

Multiplication Stories

Students were using computers in math class. They wrote stories and drew pictures to show how they solved some problems. As you read through these stories, think about what kind of pictures you would draw or what kind of stories you would write.

Their first problem was: How much is 7 × 5?

Here is the picture Jerome and Alex drew on a computer.

1. How many clouds did they draw? How many strikes of lightning did they draw?

Here is the story Jerome and Alex wrote about 7 × 5:

> We made 7 clouds. We put 5 strikes of lightning on each one.
> We found that 7 times 5 equals 35. We counted by fives 7 times.

Multiplication Stories   SG • Grade 3 • Unit 3 • Lesson 3   37

Student Guide - page 37 (Answers on p. 47)

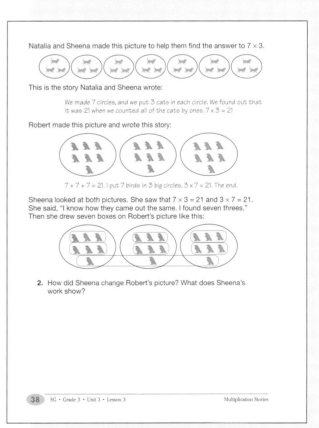

Natalia and Sheena made this picture to help them find the answer to 7 × 3.

This is the story Natalia and Sheena wrote:

> We made 7 circles, and we put 3 cats in each circle. We found out that
> it was 21 when we counted all of the cats by ones. 7 × 3 = 21

Robert made this picture and wrote this story:

> 7 + 7 + 7 = 21. I put 7 birds in 3 big circles. 3 × 7 = 21. The end.

Sheena looked at both pictures. She saw that 7 × 3 = 21 and 3 × 7 = 21. She said, "I know how they came out the same. I found seven threes." Then she drew seven boxes on Robert's picture like this:

2. How did Sheena change Robert's picture? What does Sheena's work show?

38   SG • Grade 3 • Unit 3 • Lesson 3   Multiplication Stories

Student Guide - page 38 (Answers on p. 47)

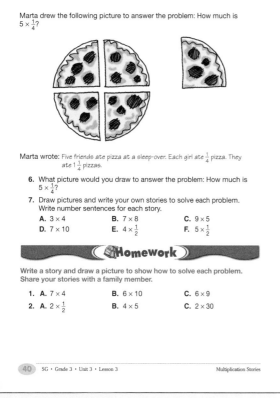

Student Guide - page 39 *(Answers on p. 48)*

3. Igor drew his picture. He solved the problem: How much is 6 × 7? Look at Igor's picture and work. How did he solve the problem?

7   7   7

7   7   7

14 + 14 + 14 = 42

Igor wrote this story:

There are six cars in the park and there are seven people in each one. 6 × 7 = 42

4. Kevin and Chanel worked on this problem: How much is 4 × 20? They used connecting cubes to solve the problem. They made four trains of cubes. How long is each train?

They divided each train into two trains of ten cubes so that they could count by tens.

10   50
20   60
30   70
40   80

5. Look at the picture. How much is 4 × 20?

Multiplication Stories   SG • Grade 3 • Unit 3 • Lesson 3   39

Math Facts

DPP Bit G develops mental math skills using subtraction facts. Bit I reminds students to practice the facts using the *Subtraction Flash Cards: Group 4.*

Homework and Practice

- DPP Task H develops number sense. For Task J, students solve problems involving time and money.
- Students write and illustrate multiplication stories for the problems listed in the Homework section of the *Student Guide.*
- Students take home the *Subtraction Flash Cards: Group 4* and list the facts they need to study so they can practice with a family member.

Assessment

Assess students' abilities to solve problems by asking them to write a story for a problem such as $8 \times \frac{1}{4}$, 10 × 9, or 20 × 3. Encourage them to draw a picture and include a number sentence.

Marta drew the following picture to answer the problem: How much is $5 \times \frac{1}{4}$?

Marta wrote: *Five friends ate pizza at a sleep-over. Each girl ate $\frac{1}{4}$ pizza. They ate $1\frac{1}{4}$ pizzas.*

6. What picture would you draw to answer the problem: How much is $5 \times \frac{1}{4}$?

7. Draw pictures and write your own stories to solve each problem. Write number sentences for each story.
   A. 3 × 4   B. 7 × 8   C. 9 × 5
   D. 7 × 10   E. $4 \times \frac{1}{2}$ F. $5 \times \frac{1}{2}$

Homework

Write a story and draw a picture to show how to solve each problem. Share your stories with a family member.

1. A. 7 × 4   B. 6 × 10   C. 6 × 9
2. A. $2 \times \frac{1}{2}$ B. 4 × 5   C. 2 × 30

40   SG • Grade 3 • Unit 3 • Lesson 3   Multiplication Stories

Student Guide - page 40 *(Answers on pp. 49–50)*

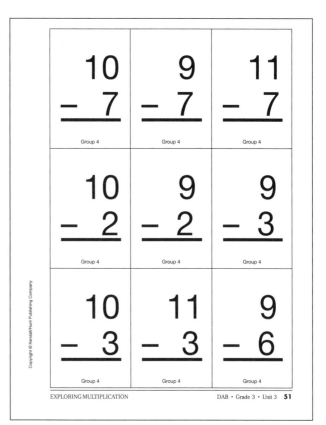

Student Guide - page 40 *(Answers on pp. 49–50)*   Discovery Assignment Book - page 51

Literature Connection

- Giganti, Paul, Jr. *Each Orange Had Eight Slices: A Counting Book.* Mulberry, New York, 1999.

This book illustrates multiplication problems with colorful drawings just as students illustrate their multiplication problems during this activity. Since the problems in this book have three factors, you can use the book to extend work with multiplication to problems with three factors.

Software Connection

- *Kid Pix* or other drawing software

If you have access to computers equipped with a drawing program, students can use them to illustrate their multiplication stories. Most examples in the *Student Guide* were drawn by second-grade students using *Kid Pix*. In the first example, two boys drew a cloud with five bolts of lightning and copied their first cloud seven times. Using the copy and paste functions in this way reinforces the operation of multiplying seven times five.

At a Glance

Math Facts and Daily Practice and Problems

DPP Bit G provides practice with subtraction facts and develops mental math skills. Task H develops number sense. Bit I reminds students to practice the subtraction facts in Group 4 using flash cards. Task J presents two time and money problems.

Teaching the Activity

1. Students read *Multiplication Stories* and discuss **Questions 1–6** in the *Student Guide.*
2. Students complete **Question 7** by writing their own multiplication stories and drawing pictures. They also write number sentences describing the problems they solve.
3. Students share their stories with the class.

Homework

1. Assign the homework problems in the *Student Guide.*
2. Students study the subtraction facts in Group 4 at home using their flash cards.

Assessment

Assess students' abilities to solve multiplication problems by asking them to write a story for a problem such as $8 \times \frac{1}{4}$, 10×9, or 20×3.

Connection

1. Use *Each Orange Had Eight Slices: A Counting Book* by Paul Giganti Jr. to extend multiplication work to problems with three factors.
2. Have students use *Kid Pix* or other drawing software to illustrate their multiplication stories.

Answer Key is on pages 47–50.

Notes:

Student Guide (p. 37)

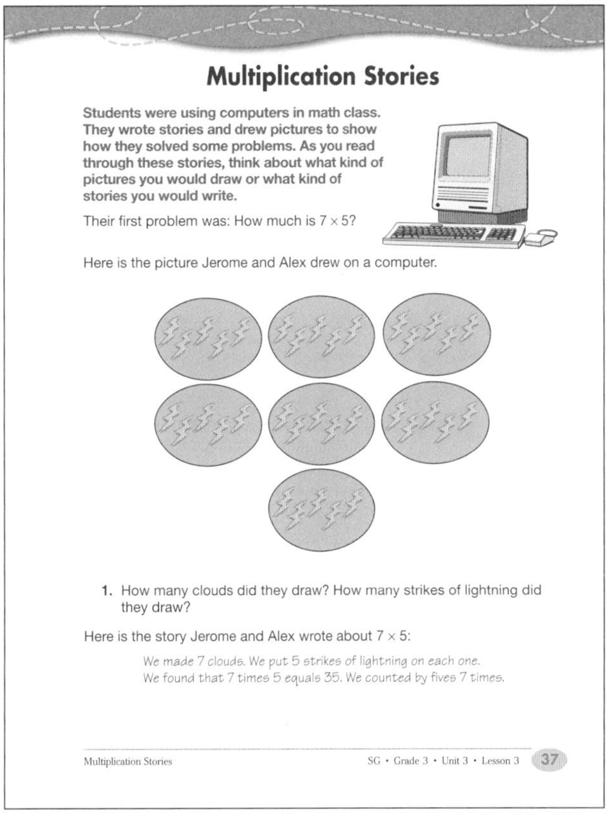

Multiplication Stories

1. 7 clouds, 35 lightning strikes

Student Guide - page 37

Student Guide (p. 38)

2. Sheena circled seven groups of three instead of three groups of seven.

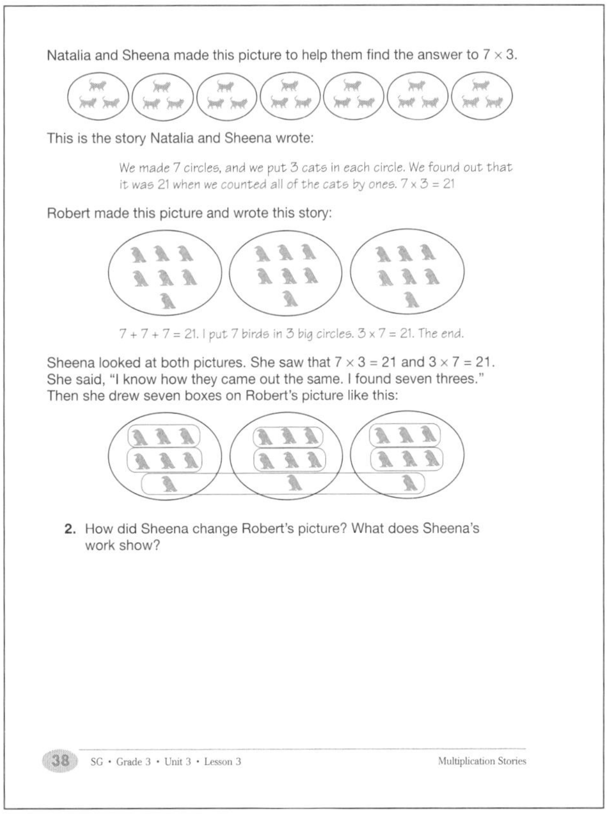

Student Guide - page 38

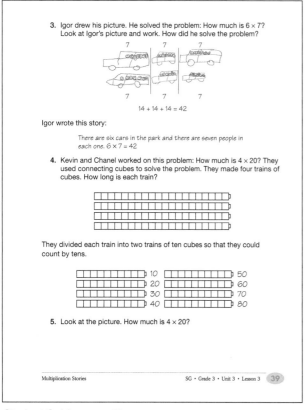

3. Igor drew his picture. He solved the problem: How much is 6 × 7? Look at Igor's picture and work. How did he solve the problem?

7   7   7

7   7   7

14 + 14 + 14 = 42

Igor wrote this story:

There are six cars in the park and there are seven people in each one. 6 × 7 = 42

4. Kevin and Chanel worked on this problem: How much is 4 × 20? They used connecting cubes to solve the problem. They made four trains of cubes. How long is each train?

They divided each train into two trains of ten cubes so that they could count by tens.

10   50
20   60
30   70
40   80

5. Look at the picture. How much is 4 × 20?

Multiplication Stories   SG • Grade 3 • Unit 3 • Lesson 3   39

Student Guide - page 39

Student Guide (p. 39)

3. Igor doubled 7 and drew three groups of fourteen people. Then he added 14 + 14 + 14 = 42.

4. 20 cubes

5. 80

Student Guide (p. 40)

6. Answers will vary. Possible picture:

7. Answers will vary. Possible stories are shown.*

A. There were three teams with four players on each. How many players were there in all?

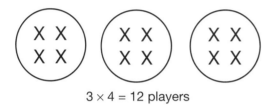

$3 \times 4 = 12$ players

B. Daisy picked seven bunches of flowers. Each bunch had eight flowers. How many flowers were there in all?

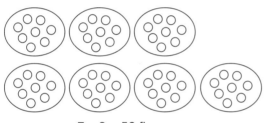

$7 \times 8 = 56$ flowers

C. There are nine houses on each of the five blocks in my neighborhood. How many houses are there in all?

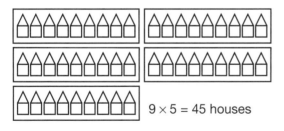

$9 \times 5 = 45$ houses

D. Jesse bought seven trays of fruit. Each tray had ten pieces of fruit. How many pieces of fruit were there altogether?

$7 \times 10 = 70$ pieces of fruit

Marta drew the following picture to answer the problem: How much is $5 \times \frac{1}{4}$?

Marta wrote: *Five friends ate pizza at a sleep-over. Each girl ate $\frac{1}{4}$ pizza. They ate $1\frac{1}{4}$ pizzas.*

6. What picture would you draw to answer the problem: How much is $5 \times \frac{1}{4}$?

7. Draw pictures and write your own stories to solve each problem. Write number sentences for each story.
A. 3×4 B. 7×8 C. 9×5
D. 7×10 E. $4 \times \frac{1}{2}$ F. $5 \times \frac{1}{2}$

Homework

Write a story and draw a picture to show how to solve each problem. Share your stories with a family member.

1. A. 7×4 B. 6×10 C. 6×9
2. A. $2 \times \frac{1}{2}$ B. 4×5 C. 2×30

40   SG • Grade 3 • Unit 3 • Lesson 3   Multiplication Stories

Student Guide - page 40

E. Kristie ate four halves of a banana. How many whole bananas did Kristie eat?

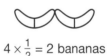

$4 \times \frac{1}{2} = 2$ bananas

F. Jong can eat five servings of rice. Each serving is one half of a plate. How many plates of rice can Jong eat?

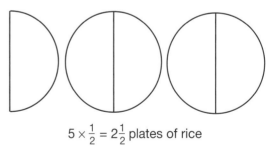

$5 \times \frac{1}{2} = 2\frac{1}{2}$ plates of rice

*Answers and/or discussion are included in the Lesson Guide.

Homework

Answers will vary. Possible stories are shown.

1. **A.** Melanie has four stickers on each of her seven notebooks. How many stickers does Melanie have in all?

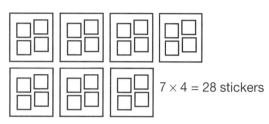 $7 \times 4 = 28$ stickers

B. There are six players on my soccer team. There are ten teams in all. How many total players are there?

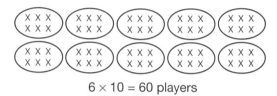

$6 \times 10 = 60$ players

C. Nine cars drove to the basketball game. There were six people in each car. How many people went to the basketball game?

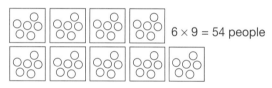 $6 \times 9 = 54$ people

2. **A.** John ate two halves of a muffin.
$2 \times \frac{1}{2} = 1$ muffin.
He ate one whole muffin.

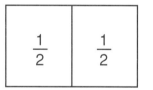

B. Rico bought five pencils for each of his 4 friends. He bought 20 pencils.

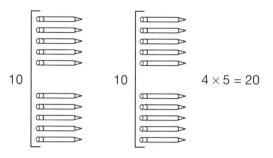

10   10 $4 \times 5 = 20$

C. There are 2 third-grade classes. Each one has 30 students.

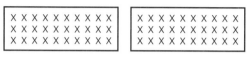

$2 \times 30 = 60$ students

Lesson 4

Making Teams

Lesson Overview

Groups of students consider the problem of dividing the class into teams of equal sizes. For each team size, they find the number of teams they can form and the number of students left over. To help solve this problem, students group counters into sets of equal sizes (with remainders). Finally, they use multiplication number sentences to represent the groupings. Although phrased in terms of multiplication, the concepts are closely related to division.

Key Content

- Dividing a set of objects into equal size groups (with remainders).
- Writing multiplication number sentences.

Math Facts

DPP Bit K develops multiplication math facts strategies.

Homework

Students complete *Groupings and Number Sentences for Ten* and the *Groupings and Number Sentences for Fifteen* Homework Pages in the *Discovery Assignment Book*.

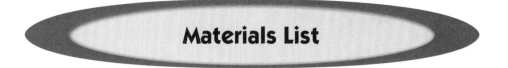

Materials List

Supplies and Copies

Student	Teacher
Supplies for Each Student • assortment of counters	**Supplies**
Copies	**Copies/Transparencies** • 1 transparency of *Class Teams Table* (*Discovery Assignment Book* Page 55)

All blackline masters including assessment, transparency, and DPP masters are also on the Teacher Resource CD.

Student Books

Class Teams Table (*Discovery Assignment Book* Page 55)
Groupings and Number Sentences for Ten (*Discovery Assignment Book* Page 57)
Groupings and Number Sentences for Fifteen (*Discovery Assignment Book* Page 58)

Daily Practice and Problems and Home Practice

DPP items K–L (*Unit Resource Guide* Pages 19–20)

Note: Classrooms whose pacing differs significantly from the suggested pacing of the units should use the Math Facts Calendar in Section 4 of the *Facts Resource Guide* to ensure students receive the complete math facts program.

Daily Practice and Problems

Suggestions for using the DPPs are on page 55.

K. Bit: Pumpkins in Wagons (URG p. 19)

This story problem was written by a third-grade student:

There are ten wagons and three pumpkins in each wagon. How many pumpkins are there? Solve the problem.

L. Challenge: Sally's and Sara's Savings (URG p. 20)

1. Sally is saving for a pair of gym shoes that cost $45. Right now she has $13. She can save $2 a week. How many weeks will Sally need to save until she has enough money for her shoes? How many months?
2. Sara wants a jump rope that costs $8. She has only $1.50 now. She can save $1 each week. How long will it be until Sara has enough money for her jump rope?

Teaching the Activity

Part 1 In Groups

You may need a large space, such as a gym, for this activity.

Call out a number and have students group themselves into teams of that size. For example:

- *Make teams of four.*

Students make teams of four. Some students may be left over. Discuss this possibility with your students. Continue by calling out other team sizes.

Part 2 Using Counters

Give each student pair the number of counters equal to the number of students in the class. Students will divide the counters into teams of various sizes. Begin with a discussion about grouping the class into teams. Ask students to investigate a team size with their counters. For many team sizes, there will be extra beans, or remainders. This activity focuses on *how many* teams of a given size are possible. A model for a classroom with twenty-six students investigating groups of six is shown in Figure 4. When the class arrives at a solution for a specific number in each team, represent it on the board.

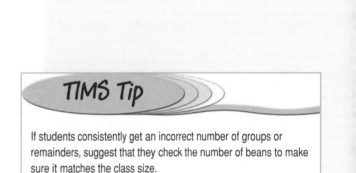

TIMS Tip

If students consistently get an incorrect number of groups or remainders, suggest that they check the number of beans to make sure it matches the class size.

Content Note

Students might order the terms in their math sentences differently. For instance, $4 \times 6 + 2 = 26$ can also be $2 + 4 \times 6 = 26$. Since multiplication is always done before addition, both expressions are correct. However, some calculators perform the operations in a left-to-right order. Thus, students might input $2 + 4 \times 6$ and receive the answer 36. If this occurs, you can help students get the correct answer by showing them how to use parentheses: $2 + (4 \times 6) = 26$. Remind them that the operation in the parentheses is done first.

Figure 4: *Four teams of six with two left over*

Name _____ Date _____

Class Teams Table

Record your class size and complete the data table.

Class size _____

Number of Teams	Team Size	Remainder	Number Sentence

Making Teams   DAB • Grade 3 • Unit 3 • Lesson 4   **55**

Discovery Assignment Book - page 55 *(Answers on p. 57)*

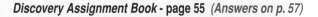

Journal Prompt

A number sentence is true if what is on one side of an equal sign has the same value as what is on the other side. Is this number sentence about three groups of four beans with two left over a true statement? $3 \times 4 = 12 + 2 = 14$ Why or why not? (No. 3×4 does not equal $12 + 2$.)

Part 3 Number Sentences

Ask students to help you write a number sentence for each model. Some students might suggest $6 + 6 + 6 + 6 + 2 = 26$ for the example in Figure 4, but you should encourage them to write a number sentence that uses multiplication: $4 \times 6 + 2 = 26$.

Work through several different team sizes as a class, before asking students to use the *Class Teams Table* Activity Page. Students should find all the possible team sizes for the class. Ask students to fill in the entries in the table's second column before they begin their investigations. Encourage the use of manipulatives to help students find and model their solutions. Students should record their findings. The data table will be complete when they have exhausted all team sizes for which they can make at least two teams. A completed table for a class of 28 students is shown in Figure 5.

You may want to guide students in organizing their lists. They could, for instance, begin with a team size of one, then consider a team size of two, and so on. If they do this, they will find it easier to see the patterns in their data. However, you may prefer to be less directive and let them discover for themselves the value of organizing data systematically.

After students finish investigating all the team sizes, they should write in their journals about the patterns they see in their data. If some students finish before others, suggest that they work on a similar problem using a different class size.

Class Size of 28

Number of Teams	Team Size	Remainder	Number Sentence
28	1	0	$28 \times 1 = 28$
14	2	0	$14 \times 2 = 28$
8	3	4	$8 \times 3 + 4 = 28$
7	4	0	$7 \times 4 = 28$
5	5	3	$5 \times 5 + 3 = 28$
4	6	4	$4 \times 6 + 4 = 28$
4	7	0	$4 \times 7 = 28$
3	8	4	$3 \times 8 + 4 = 28$
3	9	1	$3 \times 9 + 1 = 28$
2	10	8	$2 \times 10 + 8 = 28$

Figure 5: *Sample table for a class of 28 students.*

Math Facts

For DPP Bit K, students solve a word problem using multiplication.

Homework and Practice

- For DPP Challenge L, students solve problems involving time and money.

- In the *Groupings and Number Sentences for Ten* Homework Page, students practice writing multiplication sentences to describe grouping objects with remainders. This exercise is similar to playing the game of Jacks, which is described on the page. *The Groupings and Number Sentences for Fifteen* Homework Page is similar.

Literature Connection

- Slobodkina, Esphyr. *Caps for Sale: A Tale of a Peddler, Some Monkeys and Their Monkey Business.* HarperTrophy, New York, 1997.

Conduct a discussion centered around the book. Here are some suggested questions:

1. *Write number sentences to describe the number of hats in these piles:*

   a. *On the ground on the front cover.*
   $(3 \times 4 = 12)$

   b. *On the man's head on the first page.*
   $(4 \times 4 + 1 = 17)$

   c. *On the ground in the next-to-last picture in the book.* $(2 \times 4 + 3 = 11)$

2. *Caps cost 50 cents each. How much do the caps in each of the piles from Question 1 cost?*
   (a. $6.00, b. $8.50, c. $5.50)

3. *How many monkeys are there on the page that begins, "On every branch sat a monkey"? Try to answer without counting the monkeys.*
   (There are 16 hats, not counting the checked hat the man is wearing. Since there are as many monkeys as hats, there are 16 monkeys.)

Discovery Assignment Book - page 57 (Answers on p. 57)

Discovery Assignment Book - page 58 (Answers on p. 58)

At a Glance

Math Facts and Daily Practice and Problems

DPP Bit K develops multiplication math facts strategies. Challenge L presents two problems involving time and money.

Part 1. In Groups

1. Call out a number and ask students to make teams of that size.
2. Discuss the idea that some students may be left over.

Part 2. Using Counters

1. Give students counters totaling the number of students in the class.
2. Students divide the counters as they did with peers in Part 1.
3. Call out team sizes.
4. Model teams with the counters.
5. Write solutions on the board.

Part 3. Number Sentences

1. Students write a number sentence for their models.
2. Students complete the *Class Teams Table* Activity Page in the *Discovery Assignment Book.*
3. Students write in journals.
4. Students read, discuss, and answer questions about *Caps for Sale: A Tale of a Peddler, Some Monkeys and Their Monkey Business.* (optional)

Homework

Students complete *Groupings and Number Sentences for Ten* and the *Groupings and Number Sentences for Fifteen* Homework Pages in the *Discovery Assignment Book.*

Connection

Read and discuss *Caps for Sale: A Tale of a Peddler, Some Monkeys and Their Monkey Business* by Esphyr Slobodkina.

Answer Key is on pages 57–58.

Notes:

Discovery Assignment Book (p. 55)

Class Teams Table

The table will vary depending on class size and on how you choose to organize the data. *

Class Size of 28

Number of Teams	Team Size	Remainder	Number Sentence
28	1	0	$28 \times 1 = 28$
14	2	0	$14 \times 2 = 28$
8	3	4	$8 \times 3 + 4 = 28$
7	4	0	$7 \times 4 = 28$
5	5	3	$5 \times 5 + 3 = 28$
4	6	4	$4 \times 6 + 4 = 28$
4	7	0	$4 \times 7 = 28$
3	8	4	$3 \times 8 + 4 = 28$
3	9	1	$3 \times 9 + 1 = 28$
2	10	8	$2 \times 10 + 8 = 28$

Discovery Assignment Book (p. 57)

Groupings and Number Sentences for Ten

Group Size	Drawings and Words	Number Sentence
3	★ ★ ★ ★ ★ ★ ★ ★ ★ ★ 3 groups of 3 with 1 extra	$3 \times 3 + 1 = 10$
4	★ ★ ★ ★ ★ ★ ★ ★ ★ ★ 2 groups of 4 with 2 extra	$2 \times 4 + 2 = 10$
5	★ ★ ★ ★ ★ ★ ★ ★ ★ ★ 2 groups of 5 with 0 extra	$2 \times 5 + 0 = 10$
6	★ ★ ★ ★ ★ ★ ★ ★ ★ ★ 1 group of 6 with 4 extra	$1 \times 6 + 4 = 10$

Discovery Assignment Book - page 55

Discovery Assignment Book - page 57

*Answers and/or discussion are included in the Lesson Guide.

Copyright © Kendall/Hunt Publishing Company

Name _____ Date _____

Groupings and Number Sentences for Fifteen

Homework

Fill in the missing drawings, numbers, and number sentences. You will be working with fifteen as the total.

Group Size	Drawings and Words	Number Sentence
1	* * * * * * * * * * * * * * * 15 groups of 1 with 0 extra	$15 \times 1 = \underline{}$
2	** ** ** ** ** ** ** * ___ groups of 2 with ___ extra	$\underline{} \times 2 + 1 = 15$
3	*** *** *** *** *** ___ groups of 3 with ___ extra	$\underline{} \times 3 + \underline{} = 15$
4	___ groups of 4 with ___ extra	$\underline{} \times 4 + \underline{} = 15$
5	___ groups of 5 with ___ extra	
6	___ groups of 6 with ___ extra	
7	___ groups of 7 with ___ extra	
8	___ groups of 8 with ___ extra	

58   DAB • Grade 3 • Unit 3 • Lesson 4   Making Teams

Discovery Assignment Book - page 58

Discovery Assignment Book (p. 58)

Groupings and Number Sentences for Fifteen

Group Size	Drawings and Words	Number Sentence
1	15 groups of 1 with 0 extra	$15 \times 1 + 0 = 15$
2	7 groups of 2 with 1 extra	$7 \times 2 + 1 = 15$
3	5 groups of 3 with 0 extra	$5 \times 3 + 0 = 15$
4	* * * * * * * * * * * * * * * 3 groups of 4 with 3 extra	$3 \times 4 + 3 = 15$
5	* * * * * * * * * * * * * * * 3 groups of 5 with 0 extra	$3 \times 5 + 0 = 15$
6	* * * * * * * * * * * * * * * 2 groups of 6 with 3 extra	$2 \times 6 + 3 = 15$
7	* * * * * * * * * * * * * * * 2 groups of 7 with 1 extra	$2 \times 7 + 1 = 15$
8	* * * * * * * * * * * * * * * 1 group of 8 with 7 extra	$1 \times 8 + 7 = 15$

Lesson 5

Multiples on the Calendar

Lesson Overview

This ongoing activity introduces a daily routine in which students use the calendar to practice multiplication. Each month features a number: September features the number 2, October features 3, and so on. Each day, the class creates a number sentence that expresses the date as a multiple of the month's featured number plus a remainder. Introducing this activity should take one session. Afterwards, it requires only a minute or so as part of the daily routine.

Key Content

- Investigating multiples of the numbers 2 through 11.
- Representing numbers with number sentences (a product plus remainder).
- Identifying patterns.
- Using patterns to solve problems.

Key Vocabulary

- multiple

Math Facts

DPP items M and N provide math facts practice.

Homework

Assign Home Practice Part 3.

Assessment

You may use Home Practice Part 4 as an assessment. Record students' abilities to create stories for multiplication sentences and write number sentences for multiplication situations on the *Observational Assessment Record*.

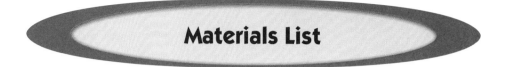

Materials List

Supplies and Copies

Student	Teacher
Supplies for Each Student • beans or other counters, optional	**Supplies** • large classroom calendar with space for writing number sentences
Copies • 1 copy of *Calendar Multiplication* per student (*Unit Resource Guide* Page 64)	**Copies/Transparencies**

All blackline masters including assessment, transparency, and DPP masters are also on the Teacher Resource CD.

Daily Practice and Problems and Home Practice

DPP items M–N (*Unit Resource Guide* Page 20)
Home Practice Parts 3–4 (*Discovery Assignment Book* Page 47)

Note: Classrooms whose pacing differs significantly from the suggested pacing of the units should use the Math Facts Calendar in Section 4 of the *Facts Resource Guide* to ensure students receive the complete math facts program.

Assessment Tools

Observational Assessment Record (*Unit Resource Guide* Pages 11–12)

Daily Practice and Problems

Suggestions for using the DPPs are on page 62.

M. Bit: Making Groups (URG p. 20) $\boxed{\frac{5}{\times 7}}$

You have thirty-seven beans. Make groups of five. Write a number sentence that shows your work. Don't forget about leftover beans.

N. Task: Subtraction Stories (URG p. 20) $\boxed{\frac{5}{\times 7}}$

1. Write a story and draw a picture for $10 - 4$.
2. Write a story and draw a picture for $11 - 4$.

Review how students wrote number sentences in Lesson 4 *Making Teams*. Discuss multiples of numbers and skip counting. A number is a **multiple** of another number if it is evenly divisible by that number. For example, 6 is a multiple of 2 since 2 divides 6 with no remainder.

- *Skip count by twos to 20.* (2, 4, 6, 8, . . .)
- *Is 4 a multiple of 2?* (Yes)
- *Is 6 a multiple of 2? Is 8 a multiple of 2?* (Yes)
- *Is 20 a multiple of 2?* (Yes)
- *What do we call numbers which are multiples of 2?* (Even numbers)

Begin with today's date and the featured number 2. Ask your class whether the date is a multiple of 2. If it is, circle it on the calendar and write a multiplication sentence using the date as the product. For example, if the date is September 20, you would write the sentence $20 = 10 \times 2$ beside the date on the calendar. If the date is not a multiple of 2, do not circle it. The number sentence you write on the calendar then will include multiplication and addition. For example, if the date is September 21, you write $21 = 10 \times 2 + 1$. Make a sentence that has the fewest number of leftover days. That is, $21 = 9 \times 2 + 3$ is mathematically correct, but $21 = 10 \times 2 + 1$ is preferred. Students can use beans or other counters to help them with this activity.

After discussing the current date, ask students to consider the days of the month that have already passed. You can work together to record the number sentences on the class calendar, or you can ask student groups to record the dates and number sentences on their individual *Calendar Multiplication* Activity Page. Let the class know you will be writing a multiplication sentence for tomorrow's date on the next day of class.

Record a number sentence daily on the calendar. When a new month begins, increase the featured number by one, and begin again. Each day, discuss the date, circle it if it is a multiple of the month's featured number, and write a number sentence using the featured number and the number of leftover days, as necessary. If you begin with 2 in September, then you will cover the factors 2 through 11 by June. Figure 6 is an example of a completed calendar for the month of October using the featured number 3.

TIMS Tip

Begin this activity on a date greater than the fifth of the month. It will be difficult for students to make the first few number sentences without first seeing examples with multiples and remainders.

TIMS Tip

You can incorporate this activity into your daily routine—perhaps in the morning as you take attendance.

Month ___October___   Featured Number ___3___

Sun	Mon	Tues	Wed	Thurs	Fri	Sat
		1 = 0×3+1	2 = 0×3+2	③ = 1×3	4 = 1×3+1	5 = 1×3+2
⑥ = 2×3	7 = 2×3+1	8 = 2×3+2	⑨ = 3×3	10 = 3×3+1	11 = 3×3+2	⑫ = 4×3
13 = 4×3+1	14 = 4×3+2	⑮ = 5×3	16 = 5×3+1	17 = 5×3+2	⑱ = 6×3	19 = 6×3+1
20 = 6×3+2	㉑ = 7×3	22 = 7×3+1	23 = 7×3+2	㉔ = 8×3	25 = 8×3+1	26 = 8×3+2
㉗ = 9×3	28 = 9×3+1	29 = 9×3+2	㉚ = 10×3	31 = 10×3+1		

Figure 6: *An example of the calendar for October using the featured number 3*

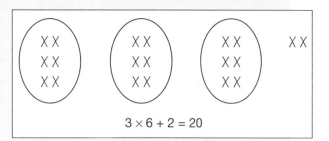

$$3 \times 6 + 2 = 20$$

Figure 7: *A multiplication picture and sentence for the date, February 20*

Although it might be helpful to introduce this activity using beans or other counters, it may not be convenient to use manipulatives on an everyday basis. As the activity progresses, you can use pictures to help students with the multiplication sentence. For example, if February's featured number is 6, draw 20 Xs on the board to show February 20, as in Figure 7.

Journal Prompt

Encourage students to write about patterns they see on the calendar as the month progresses.

Math Facts

DPP items M and N are word problems involving math facts.

Homework and Practice

Assign Home Practice Part 3. Students practice solving problems using addition facts.

Assessment

You may use Home Practice Part 4 to assess students' abilities to create stories for multiplication sentences and write number sentences for multiplication situations. Record students' progress on the *Observational Assessment Record.*

Answers for Parts 3 and 4 of the Home Practice are in the Answer Key at the end of this lesson and at the end of this unit.

Extension

Challenge students to predict the days that will be multiples of the featured number using patterns or multiplication facts. Collect and post previous months' calendars. Discuss the changing patterns. Encourage students to explain why some numbers are circled on several calendars.

Name _____ Date _____

PART 3

1. A. 60 + 40 = _____   2. A. 17 + 9 = _____
   B. 80 + 30 = _____   B. 15 + 8 = _____
   C. 70 + 90 = _____   C. 25 + 7 = _____

3. Bob saved $42 from allowances and birthday gifts. His sister said, "You saved seven more dollars than I did." How much did Bob's sister save?

   _____
   _____
   _____

PART 4

1. Write a story and draw a picture about 10 × 9. Write a number sentence about your picture.

2. You have twenty-seven stickers to share among four friends. How many stickers does each friend get? Draw a picture and use a number sentence to show how you decided.

EXPLORING MULTIPLICATION   DAB • Grade 3 • Unit 3   **47**

Discovery Assignment Book **- page 47** *(Answers on p. 65)*

Math Facts and Daily Practice and Problems

DPP items M and N provide math facts practice.

Teaching the Activity

1. Students write a number sentence with the featured number for the month and the remainder necessary to describe the date. (The featured number for September is 2, for October is 3, and so on.) For example, for September 21, students write $21 = 10 \times 2 + 1$.
2. Students write a number sentence for each day that has already passed in the month.
3. As days pass, students write a number sentence for each day.
4. Students write journal entries about patterns they see.

Homework

Assign Home Practice Part 3.

Assessment

Home Practice Part 4 can be used as an assessment. Record students' abilities to create stories for multiplication sentences and write number sentences for multiplication situations on the *Observational Assessment Record.*

Extension

Challenge students to predict the days that will be multiples of the featured number.

Answer Key is on page 65.

Notes:

Name

Calendar Multiplication

Month _____

Featured Number _____

Sunday	Monday	Tuesday	Wednesday	Thursday	Friday	Saturday

Discovery Assignment Book (p. 47)

Home Practice*

Part 3

1. **A.** 100
   B. 110
   C. 160
2. **A.** 26
   B. 23
   C. 32
3. $42.00 − $7.00 = $35.00

Part 4

1. Answers will vary.
2. Each friend will get six stickers and there will be three left over. $6 \times 4 + 3 = 27$

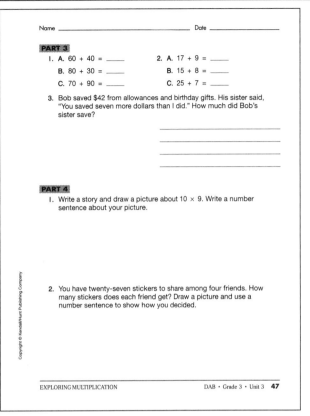

Discovery Assignment Book - page 47

Unit Resource Guide (p. 64)

Calendar Multiplication

See Lesson Guide 5 for a completed sample calendar.†

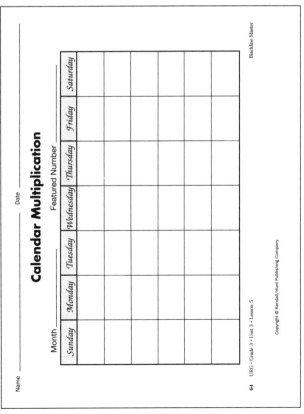

Unit Resource Guide - page 64

*Answers for all the Home Practice in the *Discovery Assignment Book* are at the end of the unit.
†Answers and/or discussion are included in the Lesson Guide.

More T-Shirt Problems

Lesson Overview

Estimated Class Sessions

1

Students solve a set of word problems using multiplication and division.

Key Content

- Solving multistep word problems involving multiplication and division.
- Communicating solutions verbally and in writing.

Math Facts

DPP Bit O provides multiplication facts practice.

Assessment

1. Use the *Observational Assessment Record* to record students' abilities to solve multiplication and division problems and explain their reasoning.
2. Transfer appropriate observations from the Unit 3 *Observational Assessment Record* to each student's *Individual Assessment Record Sheet.*

Materials List

Supplies and Copies

Student	Teacher
Supplies for Each Student • calculator • connecting cubes or other counters	**Supplies**
Copies	**Copies/Transparencies**

All blackline masters including assessment, transparency, and DPP masters are also on the Teacher Resource CD.

Student Books
More T-Shirt Problems (*Student Guide* Page 41)

Daily Practice and Problems and Home Practice
DPP items O–P (*Unit Resource Guide* Page 21)

Note: Classrooms whose pacing differs significantly from the suggested pacing of the units should use the Math Facts Calendar in Section 4 of the *Facts Resource Guide* to ensure students receive the complete math facts program.

Assessment Tools
Observational Assessment Record (*Unit Resource Guide* Pages 11–12)
Individual Assessment Record Sheet (*Teacher Implementation Guide,* Assessment section)

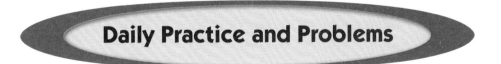

Suggestions for using the DPPs are on page 68.

O. Bit: Frank's Hamburger Stand
(URG p. 21)

A hamburger and a soda cost $5.00 at Frank's Hamburger Stand. Derek, Sean, Karl, and Cindy each ordered a hamburger and a soda. What is the total cost? Write a number sentence to show your work.

P. Challenge: Camping Trip
(URG p. 21)

The Cub Scouts are planning a camping trip. There are fifteen boys in the den. Two fathers will also go. They plan to rent four-person tents for $20 each. They will also rent two-person canoes for $10 each. What is the total cost of the canoes and tents?

More T-Shirt Problems

For each problem below, explain how you solved it.

1. There are 24 students in a class at Mann School. Every student in the class made a T-shirt with the name of the school written on it.
   A. How many letters did students have to buy to write "Mann School" on each T-shirt?
   B. The class divided into six groups to decorate the T-shirts. Each of these groups had the same number of students. How many children were in each group?

2. Ali took 20 minutes to sew the letters onto her T-shirt. Michael took three times as long. How long did Michael take?

3. Jennifer took 40 minutes to sew on her letters. Ryan took half as long. How long did Ryan take?

4. A. How many minutes are in an hour?
   B. Victoria took 1 hour and 10 minutes to sew on her letters. Emma took 25 minutes. How much longer did Victoria take than Emma?

5. Jason decorated his T-shirt with the faces of his friends. He put four faces in five rows. How many faces are on Jason's T-shirt?

6. Rosa decorated her T-shirt with flowers. She put seven flowers in three rows.
   A. How many flowers are on her T-shirt?
   B. It took Rosa 30 minutes to sew on her first row of seven flowers. How long did it take to sew all the flowers onto her T-shirt?

7. Carlita decorated her T-shirt with 20 stars. She has four rows. How many stars should she put in each row?

8. The Mann School marching band has 5 students in a row and six rows. How many students are in the band?

More T-Shirt Problems   SG · Grade 3 · Unit 3 · Lesson 6   41

Student Guide - page 41 (Answers on p. 70)

Teaching the Activity

Students can work on these problems individually, in pairs, or in groups. Students may complete them all at once or you can distribute them throughout the unit. Create additional problems as needed or encourage the students to write their own.

Although these problems involve multiplication and division, students should still be encouraged to use strategies such as skip counting, using manipulatives, and drawing pictures. Continue to model the connection between these problems and multiplication number sentences.

Math Facts

DPP Bit O is a word problem that provides math facts practice.

Homework and Practice

DPP Challenge P is a problem involving money.

Assessment

Any of the problems from the *More T-Shirt Problems* Activity Page can be used to assess students' abilities to solve multiplication and division problems and explain their reasoning. Note students' progress on the *Observational Assessment Record*. Transfer appropriate documentation from the Unit 3 *Observational Assessment Record* to the students' *Individual Assessment Record Sheets*.

Extension

Ask students to write their own problems involving multiplication and division. Have students swap problems with a partner. After partners solve their partners' problems they can check each other's solutions and strategies.

At a Glance

Math Facts and Daily Practice and Problems

DPP Bit O provides multiplication facts practice and Challenge P provides practice with money.

Teaching the Activity

1. Students solve **Questions 1–8** on the *More T-Shirt Problems* Activity Page in the *Student Guide*. They can work individually or in small groups. Calculators and counters or connecting cubes should be available.
2. Students discuss their solution strategies with the class.

Assessment

1. Use the *Observational Assessment Record* to record students' abilities to solve multiplication and division problems and explain their reasoning.
2. Transfer appropriate observations from the Unit 3 *Observational Assessment Record* to each student's *Individual Assessment Record Sheet*.

Extension

Have students write their own multiplication and division problems and then challenge a classmate to solve their problems.

Answer Key is on page 70.

Notes:

More T-Shirt Problems

For each problem below, explain how you solved it.

1. There are 24 students in a class at Mann School. Every student in the class made a T-shirt with the name of the school written on it.

   A. How many letters did students have to buy to write "Mann School" on each T-shirt?

   B. The class divided into six groups to decorate the T-shirts. Each of these groups had the same number of students. How many children were in each group?

2. Ali took 20 minutes to sew the letters onto her T-shirt. Michael took three times as long. How long did Michael take?

3. Jennifer took 40 minutes to sew on her letters. Ryan took half as long. How long did Ryan take?

4. A. How many minutes are in an hour?

   B. Victoria took 1 hour and 10 minutes to sew on her letters. Emma took 25 minutes. How much longer did Victoria take than Emma?

5. Jason decorated his T-shirt with the faces of his friends. He put four faces in five rows. How many faces are on Jason's T-shirt?

6. Rosa decorated her T-shirt with flowers. She put seven flowers in three rows.

   A. How many flowers are on her T-shirt?

   B. It took Rosa 30 minutes to sew on her first row of seven flowers. How long did it take to sew all the flowers onto her T-shirt?

7. Carlita decorated her T-shirt with 20 stars. She has four rows. How many stars should she put in each row?

8. The Mann School marching band has 5 students in a row and six rows. How many students are in the band?

More T-Shirt Problems   SG • Grade 3 • Unit 3 • Lesson 6   41

Student Guide - page 41

Student Guide (p. 41)

1. A. 240 letters*

   B. 4 children*

2. 60 minutes or 1 hour

3. 20 minutes

4. A. 60 minutes

   B. 45 minutes

5. 20 faces*

6. A. 21 flowers*

   B. 90 minutes or 1 hour 30 minutes*

7. 5 stars*

8. 30 students

*Answers and/or discussion are included in the Lesson Guide.

Discovery Assignment Book (p. 46)

Part 1

1. **A.** 4
   B. 4
   C. 8
2. **A.** 40
   B. 40
   C. 80
3. $24 - 16 = 8$ people

Part 2

Strategies will vary.

1. $5 \times 4 = 20$ letters
2. $20 \times \$0.10 = \$2.00$

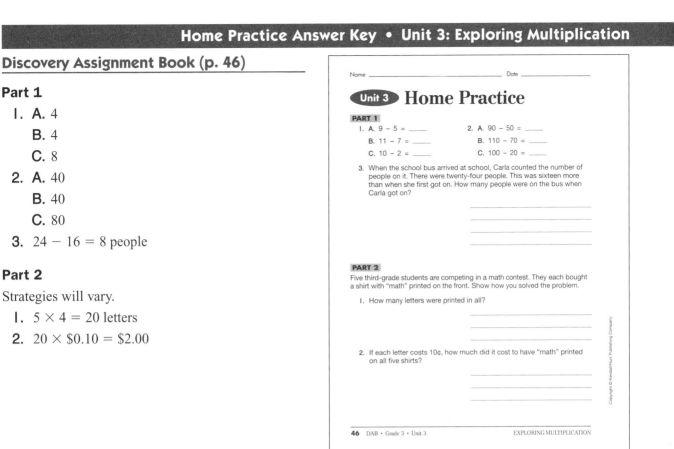

Discovery Assignment Book - page 46

Discovery Assignment Book (p. 47)

Part 3

1. **A.** 100
   B. 110
   C. 160
2. **A.** 26
   B. 23
   C. 32
3. $\$42.00 - \$7.00 = \$35.00$

Part 4

1. Answers will vary.
2. Each friend will get six stickers and there will be three left over. $6 \times 4 + 3 = 27$

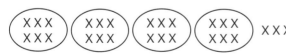

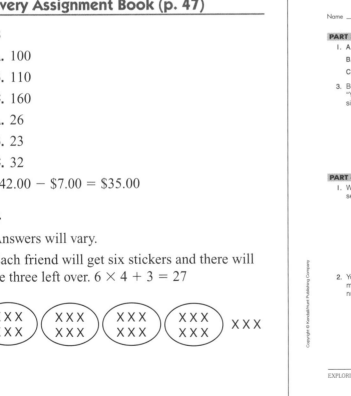

Discovery Assignment Book - page 47

*Answers and/or discussion are included in the Lesson Guide.

Glossary

This glossary provides definitions of key vocabulary terms in the Grade 3 lessons. Locations of key vocabulary terms in the curriculum are included with each definition. Components Key: URG = *Unit Resource Guide,* SG = *Student Guide,* and DAB = *Discovery Assignment Book.*

A

Area (URG Unit 5; SG Unit 5)
The area of a shape is the amount of space it covers, measured in square units.

Array (URG Unit 7 & Unit 11)
An array is an arrangement of elements into a rectangular pattern of (horizontal) rows and (vertical) columns. (*See* column and row.)

Associative Property of Addition (URG Unit 2)
For any three numbers *a, b,* and *c* we have $a + (b + c) = (a + b) + c$. For example in finding the sum of 4, 8, and 2, one can compute $4 + 8$ first and then add 2: $(4 + 8) + 2 = 14$. Alternatively, we can compute $8 + 2$ and then add the result to 4: $4 + (8 + 2) = 4 + 10 = 14$.

Average (URG Unit 5)
A number that can be used to represent a typical value in a set of data. (*See also* mean and median.)

Axes (URG Unit 8; SG Unit 8)
Reference lines on a graph. In the Cartesian coordinate system, the axes are two perpendicular lines that meet at the origin. The singular of axes is axis.

B

Base (of a cube model) (URG Unit 18; SG Unit 18)
The part of a cube model that sits on the "ground."

Base-Ten Board (URG Unit 4)
A tool to help children organize base-ten pieces when they are representing numbers.

Base-Ten Pieces (URG Unit 4; SG Unit 4)
A set of manipulatives used to model our number system as shown in the figure at the right. Note that a skinny is made of 10 bits, a flat is made of 100 bits, and a pack is made of 1000 bits.

Base-Ten Shorthand (SG Unit 4)
A pictorial representation of the base-ten pieces as shown.

Nickname	Picture	Shorthand
bit		•
skinny		/
flat		
pack		

Best-Fit Line (URG Unit 9; SG Unit 9; DAB Unit 9)
The line that comes closest to the most number of points on a point graph.

Bit (URG Unit 4; SG Unit 4)
A cube that measures 1 cm on each edge. It is the smallest of the base-ten pieces that is often used to represent 1. (*See also* base-ten pieces.)

C

Capacity (URG Unit 16)
1. The volume of the inside of a container.
2. The largest volume a container can hold.

Cartesian Coordinate System (URG Unit 8)
A method of locating points on a flat surface by means of numbers. This method is named after its originator, René Descartes. (*See also* coordinates.)

Centimeter (cm)
A unit of measure in the metric system equal to one-hundredth of a meter. (1 inch = 2.54 cm)

Column (URG Unit 11)
In an array, the objects lined up vertically.

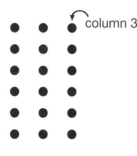

Common Fraction (URG Unit 15)
Any fraction that is written with a numerator and denominator that are whole numbers. For example, $\frac{3}{4}$ and $\frac{9}{4}$ are both common fractions. (*See also* decimal fraction.)

Commutative Property of Addition (URG Unit 2 & Unit 11)
This is also known as the Order Property of Addition. Changing the order of the addends does not change the sum. For example, $3 + 5 = 5 + 3 = 8$. Using variables, $n + m = m + n$.

Commutative Property of Multiplication (URG Unit 11)
Changing the order of the factors in a multiplication problem does not change the result, e.g., $7 \times 3 = 3 \times 7 = 21$. (*See also* turn-around facts.)

Congruent (URG Unit 12 & Unit 17; SG Unit 12)
Figures with the same shape and size.

Convenient Number (URG Unit 6)
A number used in computation that is close enough to give a good estimate, but is also easy to compute mentally, e.g., 25 and 30 are convenient numbers for 27.

Coordinates (URG Unit 8; SG Unit 8)
An ordered pair of numbers that locates points on a flat surface by giving distances from a pair of coordinate axes. For example, if a point has coordinates (4, 5) it is 4 units from the vertical axis and 5 units from the horizontal axis.

Counting Back (URG Unit 2)
A strategy for subtracting in which students start from a larger number and then count down until the number is reached. For example, to solve $8 - 3$, begin with 8 and count down three, 7, 6, 5.

Counting Down (*See* counting back.)

Counting Up (URG Unit 2)
A strategy for subtraction in which the student starts at the lower number and counts on to the higher number. For example, to solve $8 - 5$, the student starts at 5 and counts up three numbers (6, 7, 8). So $8 - 5 = 3$.

Cube (SG Unit 18)
A three-dimensional shape with six congruent square faces.

Cubic Centimeter (cc)
(URG Unit 16; SG Unit 16)
The volume of a cube that is one centimeter long on each edge.

cubic centimeter

Cup (URG Unit 16)
A unit of volume equal to 8 fluid ounces, one-half pint.

D

Decimal Fraction (URG Unit 15)
A fraction written as a decimal. For example, 0.75 and 0.4 are decimal fractions and $\frac{75}{100}$ and $\frac{4}{10}$ are called common fractions. (*See also* fraction.)

Denominator (URG Unit 13)
The number below the line in a fraction. The denominator indicates the number of equal parts in which the unit whole is divided. For example, the 5 is the denominator in the fraction $\frac{2}{5}$. In this case the unit whole is divided into five equal parts.

Density (URG Unit 16)
The ratio of an object's mass to its volume.

Difference (URG Unit 2)
The answer to a subtraction problem.

Dissection (URG Unit 12 & Unit 17)
Cutting or decomposing a geometric shape into smaller shapes that cover it exactly.

Distributive Property of Multiplication over Addition (URG Unit 19)
For any three numbers *a, b,* and *c, a* × (*b* + *c*) = *a* × *b* + *a* × *c.* The distributive property is the foundation for most methods of multidigit multiplication. For example, $9 \times (17) = 9 \times (10 + 7) = 9 \times 10 + 9 \times 7 = 90 + 63 = 153$.

E

Equal-Arm Balance
See two-pan balance.

Equilateral Triangle (URG Unit 7)
A triangle with all sides of equal length and all angles of equal measure.

Equivalent Fractions (SG Unit 17)
Fractions that have the same value, e.g., $\frac{2}{4} = \frac{1}{2}$.

Estimate (URG Unit 5 & Unit 6)
1. (verb) To find *about* how many.
2. (noun) An approximate number.

Extrapolation (URG Unit 7)
Using patterns in data to make predictions or to estimate values that lie beyond the range of values in the set of data.

F

Fact Family (URG Unit 11; SG Unit 11)
Related math facts, e.g., $3 \times 4 = 12$, $4 \times 3 = 12$, $12 \div 3 = 4$, $12 \div 4 = 3$.

Factor (URG Unit 11; SG Unit 11)
1. In a multiplication problem, the numbers that are multiplied together. In the problem $3 \times 4 = 12$, 3 and 4 are the factors.
2. Whole numbers that can be multiplied together to get a number. That is, numbers that divide a number evenly, e.g., 1, 2, 3, 4, 6, and 12 are all the factors of 12.

Fewest Pieces Rule (URG Unit 4 & Unit 6; SG Unit 4)
Using the least number of base-ten pieces to represent a number. (*See also* base-ten pieces.)

Flat (URG Unit 4; SG Unit 4)
A block that measures 1 cm $\times$ 10 cm $\times$ 10 cm. It is one of the base-ten pieces that is often used to represent 100. (*See also* base-ten pieces.)

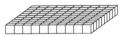

Flip (URG Unit 12)
A motion of the plane in which a figure is reflected over a line so that any point and its image are the same distance from the line.

Fraction (URG Unit 15)
A number that can be written as $\frac{a}{b}$ where a and b are whole numbers and b is not zero. For example, $\frac{1}{2}$, 0.5, and 2 are all fractions since 0.5 can be written as $\frac{5}{10}$ and 2 can be written as $\frac{2}{1}$.

Front-End Estimation (URG Unit 6)
Estimation by looking at the left-most digit.

G

Gallon (gal) (URG Unit 16)
A unit of volume equal to four quarts.

Gram
The basic unit used to measure mass.

H

Hexagon (SG Unit 12)
A six-sided polygon.

Horizontal Axis (SG Unit 1)
In a coordinate grid, the *x*-axis. The axis that extends from left to right.

I

Interpolation (URG Unit 7)
Making predictions or estimating values that lie between data points in a set of data.

J

K

Kilogram
1000 grams.

L

Likely Event (SG Unit 1)
An event that has a high probability of occurring.

Line of Symmetry (URG Unit 12)
A line is a line of symmetry for a plane figure if, when the figure is folded along this line, the two parts match exactly.

Line Symmetry (URG Unit 12; SG Unit 12)
A figure has line symmetry if it has at least one line of symmetry.

Liter (l) (URG Unit 16; SG Unit 16)
Metric unit used to measure volume. A liter is a little more than a quart.

M

Magic Square (URG Unit 2)
A square array of digits in which the sums of the rows, columns, and main diagonals are the same.

Making a Ten (URG Unit 2)
Strategies for addition and subtraction that make use of knowing the sums to ten. For example, knowing $6 + 4 = 10$ can be helpful in finding $10 - 6 = 4$ and $11 - 6 = 5$.

Mass (URG Unit 9 & Unit 16; SG Unit 9)
The amount of matter in an object.

Mean (URG Unit 5)
An average of a set of numbers that is found by adding the values of the data and dividing by the number of values.

Measurement Division (URG Unit 7)
Division as equal grouping. The total number of objects and the number of objects in each group are known. The number of groups is the unknown. For example, tulip bulbs come in packages of 8. If 216 bulbs are sold, how many packages are sold?

Measurement Error (URG Unit 9)
The unavoidable error that occurs due to the limitations inherent to any measurement instrument.

Median (URG Unit 5; DAB Unit 5)
For a set with an odd number of data arranged in order, it is the middle number. For an even number of data arranged in order, it is the number halfway between the two middle numbers.

Meniscus (URG Unit 16; SG Unit 16)
The curved surface formed when a liquid creeps up the side of a container (for example, a graduated cylinder).

Meter (m)
The standard unit of length measure in the metric system. One meter is approximately 39 inches.

Milliliter (ml) (URG Unit 16; SG Unit 16)
A measure of capacity in the metric system that is the volume of a cube that is one centimeter long on each edge.

Multiple (URG Unit 3 & Unit 11)
A number is a multiple of another number if it is evenly divisible by that number. For example, 12 is a multiple of 2 since 2 divides 12 evenly.

N

Numerator (URG Unit 13)
The number written above the line in a fraction. For example, the 2 is the numerator in the fraction $\frac{2}{5}$. (*See also* denominator.)

O

One-Dimensional Object (URG Unit 18; SG Unit 18)
An object is one-dimensional if it is made up of pieces of lines and curves.

Ordered Pairs (URG Unit 8)
A pair of numbers that gives the coordinates of a point on a grid in relation to the origin. The horizontal coordinate is given first; the vertical coordinate is given second. For example, the ordered pair (5, 3) tells us to move five units to the right of the origin and 3 units up.

Origin (URG Unit 8)
The point at which the *x*- and *y*-axes (horizontal and vertical axes) intersect on a coordinate plane. The origin is described by the ordered pair (0, 0) and serves as a reference point so that all the points on the plane can be located by ordered pairs.

P

Pack (URG Unit 4; SG Unit 4)
A cube that measures 10 cm on each edge. It is one of the base-ten pieces that is often used to represent 1000. (*See also* base-ten pieces.)

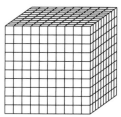

Palindrome (URG Unit 6)
A number, word, or phrase that reads the same forward and backward, e.g., 12321.

Parallel Lines (URG Unit 18)
Lines that are in the same direction. In the plane, parallel lines are lines that do not intersect.

Parallelogram (URG Unit 18)
A quadrilateral with two pairs of parallel sides.

Partitive Division (URG Unit 7)
Division as equal sharing. The total number of objects and the number of groups are known. The number of objects in each group is the unknown. For example, Frank has 144 marbles that he divides equally into 6 groups. How many marbles are in each group?

Pentagon (SG Unit 12)
A five-sided, five-angled polygon.

Perimeter (URG Unit 7; DAB Unit 7)
The distance around a two-dimensional shape.

Pint (URG Unit 16)
A unit of volume measure equal to 16 fluid ounces, i.e., two cups.

Polygon
A two-dimensional connected figure made of line segments in which each endpoint of every side meets with an endpoint of exactly one other side.

Population (URG Unit 1; SG Unit 1)
A collection of persons or things whose properties will be analyzed in a survey or experiment.

Prediction (SG Unit 1)
Using data to declare or foretell what is likely to occur.

Prime Number (URG Unit 11)
A number that has exactly two factors. For example, 7 has exactly two distinct factors, 1 and 7.

Prism
A three-dimensional figure that has two congruent faces, called bases, that are parallel to each other, and all other faces are parallelograms.

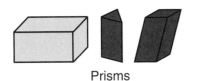

Prisms   Not a prism

Product (URG Unit 11; SG Unit 11; DAB Unit 11)
The answer to a multiplication problem. In the problem $3 \times 4 = 12$, 12 is the product.

Q

Quadrilateral (URG Unit 18)
A polygon with four sides.

Quart (URG Unit 16)
A unit of volume equal to 32 fluid ounces; one quarter of a gallon.

R

Recording Sheet (URG Unit 4)
A place value chart used for addition and subtraction problems.

Rectangular Prism (URG Unit 18; SG Unit 18)
A prism whose bases are rectangles. A right rectangular prism is a prism having all faces rectangles.

Regular (URG Unit 7; DAB Unit 7)
A polygon is regular if all sides are of equal length and all angles are equal.

Remainder (URG Unit 7)
Something that remains or is left after a division problem. The portion of the dividend that is not evenly divisible by the divisor, e.g., $16 \div 5 = 3$ with 1 as a remainder.

Right Angle (SG Unit 12)
An angle that measures 90°.

Rotation (turn) (URG Unit 12)
A transformation (motion) in which a figure is turned a specified angle and direction around a point.

Row (URG Unit 11)
In an array, the objects lined up horizontally.

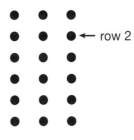

Rubric (URG Unit 2)
A written guideline for assigning scores to student work, for the purpose of assessment.

S

Sample (URG Unit 1; SG Unit 1)
A part or subset of a population.

Skinny (URG Unit 4; SG Unit 4)
A block that measures 1 cm $\times$ 1 cm $\times$ 10 cm. It is one of the base-ten pieces that is often used to represent 10. (*See also* base-ten pieces.)

Square Centimeter (sq cm) (SG Unit 5)
The area of a square that is 1 cm long on each side.

Square Number (SG Unit 11)
A number that is the product of a whole number multiplied by itself. For example, 25 is a square number since $5 \times 5 = 25$. A square number can be represented by a square array with the same number of rows as columns. A square array for 25 has 5 rows of 5 objects in each row or 25 total objects.

Standard Masses
A set of objects with convenient masses, usually 1 g, 10 g, 100 g, etc.

Sum (URG Unit 2; SG Unit 2)
The answer to an addition problem.

Survey (URG Unit 14; SG Unit 14)
An investigation conducted by collecting data from a sample of a population and then analyzing it. Usually surveys are used to make predictions about the entire population.

T

Tangrams (SG Unit 12)
A type of geometric puzzle. A shape is given and it must be covered exactly with seven standard shapes called tans.

Thinking Addition (URG Unit 2)
A strategy for subtraction that uses a related addition problem. For example, $15 - 7 = 8$ because $8 + 7 = 15$.

Three-Dimensional (URG Unit 18; SG Unit 18)
Existing in three-dimensional space; having length, width, and depth.

TIMS Laboratory Method (URG Unit 1; SG Unit 1)
A method that students use to organize experiments and investigations. It involves four components: draw, collect, graph, and explore. It is a way to help students learn about the scientific method.

Turn (URG Unit 12)
(*See* rotation.)

Turn-Around Facts (URG Unit 2 & Unit 11 p. 37; SG Unit 11)
Addition facts that have the same addends but in a different order, e.g., $3 + 4 = 7$ and $4 + 3 = 7$. (*See also* commutative property of addition and commutative property of multiplication.)

Two-Dimensional (URG Unit 18; SG Unit 18)
Existing in the plane; having length and width.

Two-Pan Balance
A device for measuring the mass of an object by balancing the object against a number of standard masses (usually multiples of 1 unit, 10 units, and 100 units, etc.).

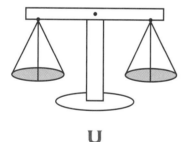

U

Unit (of measurement) (URG Unit 18)
A precisely fixed quantity used to measure. For example, centimeter, foot, kilogram, and quart are units of measurement.

Using a Ten (URG Unit 2)
1. A strategy for addition that uses partitions of the number 10. For example, one can find $8 + 6$ by thinking $8 + 6 = 8 + 2 + 4 = 10 + 4 = 14$.
2. A strategy for subtraction that uses facts that involve subtracting 10. For example, students can use $17 - 10 = 7$ to learn the "close fact" $17 - 9 = 8$.

Using Doubles (URG Unit 2)
Strategies for addition and subtraction that use knowing doubles. For example, one can find $7 + 8$ by thinking $7 + 8 = 7 + 7 + 1 = 14 + 1 = 15$. Knowing $7 + 7 = 14$ can be helpful in finding $14 - 7 = 7$ and $14 - 8 = 6$.

V

Value (URG Unit 1; SG Unit 1)
The possible outcomes of a variable. For example, red, green, and blue are possible values for the variable *color*. Two meters and 1.65 meters are possible values for the variable *length*.

Variable (URG Unit 1; SG Unit 1)
1. An attribute or quantity that changes or varies.
2. A symbol that can stand for a variable.

Vertex (URG Unit 12; SG Unit 12)
1. A point where the sides of a polygon meet.
2. A point where the edges of a three-dimensional object meet.

Vertical Axis (SG Unit 1)
In a coordinate grid, the *y*-axis. It is perpendicular to the horizontal axis.

Volume (URG Unit 16; SG Unit 16)
The measure of the amount of space occupied by an object.

Volume by Displacement (URG Unit 16)
A way of measuring volume of an object by measuring the amount of water (or some other fluid) it displaces.

W

Weight (URG Unit 9)
A measure of the pull of gravity on an object. One unit for measuring weight is the pound.

X

Y

Z